THE Shift CODE

Your Personal Empowerment Masterplan

Gay Page

READERS AND EXPERTS RAVE ABOUT THE SHIFT CODE

I learned to drive on a stick SHIFT. By learning how to SHIFT, I could get to where I wanted to go. This comprehensive and inspiring book does just that. If you follow its daily routine, you will get to where you want to go. Gay Page has travelled the journey and knows the territory well. She shares this with us and makes the journey more enjoyable with her breadth of knowledge and wisdom. Gay is a trustworthy and reliable guide so enjoy the journey. Happy trails and remember—SHIFT happens.

— *Rev. Janet Stangvik*

As a physician and psychiatrist, I have witnessed countless unexpected and unimaginable "miracles." Many of these miracles seem to lie outside the boundaries of modern medicine, technology, and pharmaceuticals, even while utilizing all of these. These 'miracles" are not dependent on age, condition, intellect, or education. Some are profound, some subtle, many go unnoticed. Many are relayed by "chance" meetings in everyday life and travel through these encounters throughout time. Trust, faith, and openness, to the holistic truth about ourselves, our life, and our path ahead appear to be key ingredients. We all can find ourselves in a bottleneck along the way. All of us need assistance from time to time to jump start us out of our unhealthy patterns in order to begin and embrace a new level of personal awakening for this leg of our journey. We need a guide.

The Shift Code is just such a guide. *The Shift Code* is a well-designed blueprint for increasing self-understanding, with the bonus of reaching you wherever you are. This book serves as a masterplan for an organized journey of self-discovery in a very approachable workbook format.
I am grateful this book came my way. Begin to learn *The Shift Code* and start your own journey of self-discovery!

— *M. Fiorella, DO, ABHIM*

The joy of learning. The joy of doing. You will have both upon reading *The Shift Code: Your Personal Empowerment Masterplan* by Gay Page. *The Shift Code* is more than a "self-help" book. The author educates, encourages, and provides the reader with an organized plan for self-understanding and—if needed—ideas for change. A perfect workbook for anyone interested in becoming aware of what creates their worldview and how to transform negativity into a flourishing life of gratitude and positivity.

— *Vera M. Holder, MA*
Professor Emeritus and Communication Consultant

According to research published in *The Harvard Business Review*, successful CEOs spend about 15% of their time reading. True, much of any CEOs reading time relates to improving business acumen but improving effective communication skills and emotional intelligence cannot be overstated. The author's extensive leadership and teaching experiences are intertwined in *The Shift Code: Your Personal Improvement Masterplan*. We have incorporated this book as a catalyst for team building. Team members report the segments on resilience, integrity, and emotional intelligence provide powerful tools both inside and out of a professional environment. I encourage anyone in a leadership position to have *The Shift Code* be a part of their daily read.

— Robert J. Crutchfield, MS
Founder and CEO, The Interfield Group

Having taught collegiate-level interpersonal, intrapersonal, and small group communication studies for over 30 years, I can attest that *The Shift Code: Your Personal Empowerment Masterplan* is a perfect companion reader for courses in the field of communication studies. Understanding the self is critical in improving communication with others. Read it. Try it. You won't be disappointed.

— Stephanie Fondren, MA
Professor Communication Studies, Professional Speaker, and Seminar Leader

This book is a ray of sunshine on every page. The author cheers you on with contagious enthusiasm and guides you with a daily plan to discover your dreams and manifest your Destiny. Well worth the journey.

— Sage Bennet, Ph.D.
Author of *Wisdom Walk: Nine Practices to Create Peace and Balance from the World Spiritual Traditions*

If you're grappling with negative thoughts about life and questioning where you fit in, *The Shift Code* is the book you've been waiting for! This one-of-a-kind workbook is designed to help you uncover your unique strengths and tackle areas for growth, empowering you to create meaningful change in your life.

Drawing from my experience as an activist in social movements such as LGBTQ+ Safe Space, I Am Equality, the NOH8 Campaign, and Thrive: People Like Us!, I've seen firsthand how self-awareness can be a transformative tool. Embracing love, forgiveness, and genuine joy has been essential in my own journey and can be equally impactful for you. These powerful tools will guide you toward success as you navigate life's challenges with newfound confidence and purpose.

— Lance R. Lockwood
Professor and Distinguished Faculty, Author, and Activist

THE Shift CODE

Your Personal Empowerment Masterplan

S SPIRIT

H HOLDS

I INSPIRATION

F FOR

T TRANSFORMATION

Copywrite © 2024 by Virginia Gay Page

ALL RIGHTS RESERVED

No part of this book may be translated, used, or reproduced in any form or by any means, in whole or in part, electronic or mechanical, including photocopying, recording, taping, or by any information storage or retrieval system without express written permission from the author or the publisher, except for the use in brief quotations within critical articles and reviews.

Limits of Liability and Disclaimer of Warranty:

The author and publisher shall not be liable for your misuse of this material. The contents are strictly for informational and educational purposes only.

Warning – Disclaimer:

The purpose of this book is to educate and entertain. The author and/or publisher do not guarantee that anyone following these techniques, suggestions, tips, ideas, or strategies will become successful. The author and/or publisher shall have neither liability nor responsibility to anyone with respect to loss or damage caused, or alleged to be caused, directly or indirectly by the information contained in this book. Further, readers should be aware that Internet websites listed in this work may have changed or disappeared between when this work was written and when it was read.

Printed and bound in the United States of America

ISBN: 979-8-9920336-0-1

Book Cover and Graphic Design by Susan Rhyne

DEDICATION

To Vivian for her strength and unequivocal belief in me.

To Vera for her brilliance, encouragement, and friendship.

CONTENTS

Foreword

Preface

Introduction

Daily Guide and Workbook

Week One	Who Am I?	1
	Daily Routine Checklist	3
	1 My Dream!	4
	2 My Interests and Talents	6
	3 My Roles in Life	8
	4 My Core Values	10
	5 My Strengths and Weaknesses	12
	6 My Support Team	14
	7 My Personal Mission Statement	16
Week Two	Becoming the Master of My Shift!	19
	Daily Routine Checklist	21
	1 Wake Up!	22
	2 Identify Negative Patterns	24
	3 Challenge Negative Thoughts	26
	4 Reframe Negative Thoughts	28
	5 Mindfulness	30
	6 Activate and Engage	32
	7 Consistency and Persistence	34
Week Three	The Orchard in Your Mind	37
	Daily Routine Checklist	39
	1 Plan	40
	2 Prepare the Soil	42
	3 Plant the Seeds	44
	4 Feed	46
	5 Observe	48
	6 Tend and Weed	50
	7 Celebrate the Feast!	52
Week Four	Mindfulness	55
	Daily Routine Checklist	57
	1 Conscious Presence	58
	2 Intention	60
	3 Patience	62
	4 Attitude	64
	5 Open Mind	66
	6 Self Compassion	68
	7 Release	70

CONTENTS

Week Five	Resilience		73
	Daily Routine Checklist		75
	1	Elasticity	76
	2	Lifestyle	78
	3	Relationship Ecosystem	80
	4	Time Management	82
	5	Illumination	84
	6	Balancing the Pendulum	86
	7	Self-Talk	88
Week Six	Kindness		91
	Daily Routine Checklist		93
	1	Kindness 101	94
	2	What if I …?	96
	3	Empathy	98
	4	Testing … Testing	100
	5	Authenticity	102
	6	Circulation	104
	7	Random Acts of Kindness	106
Week Seven	Gratitude		109
	Daily Routine Checklist		111
	1	Mindset	112
	2	Mother Nature	114
	3	Relationships	116
	4	Achievements	118
	5	Needs versus Wants	120
	6	Adventures	122
	7	Exploration	124
Week Eight	Forgiveness		127
	Daily Routine Checklist		129
	1	Acknowledge	130
	2	Understand	132
	3	Accept Responsibility	134
	4	Release Resentment	136
	5	Heal	138
	6	Set Boundaries	140
	7	Forgiveness Pledge	142
Week Nine	Humility		145
	Daily Routine Checklist		147
	1	Self-Awareness	148
	2	Open to Feedback	150
	3	Appreciation	152
	4	Respect for Others	154
	5	Community Service	156
	6	Adaptability	158
	7	Self-Reflection	160

CONTENTS

Week Ten	Integrity		163
	Daily Routine Checklist		165
	1	Honesty	166
	2	Trustworthy	168
	3	Ethics	170
	4	Competence	172
	5	Transparency	174
	6	Loyalty	176
	7	Accountability	178
Week Eleven	Emotional Intelligence		181
	Daily Routine Checklist		183
	1	Inner Consciousness	184
	2	Body Language	186
	3	Cerebral Blueprint	188
	4	Behavioral Blueprint	190
	5	Communication	192
	6	Tact	194
	7	Diplomacy	196
Week Twelve	Spirituality		199
	Daily Routine Checklist		201
	1	Belief	202
	2	Faith	204
	3	Trust	206
	4	Hope	208
	5	Vulnerability	210
	6	Intuition	212
	7	Spirit	214
Week Thirteen	Connectedness		217
	Daily Routine Checklist		219
	1	Love	220
	2	Belonging	222
	3	Purpose	224
	4	Grace	226
	5	Joy	228
	6	Peace	230
	7	Unity	232
Week Fourteen	Life		235
	Daily Routine Checklist		237
	1	Awe	238
	2	Curiosity	240
	3	Humor	242
	4	Passion	244
	5	Endurance	246
	6	Abundance	248
	7	Zest	250

CONTENTS

Week Fifteen	Who Am I Now?	253
	Daily Routine Checklist	255
	1 My Dream!	256
	2 My Interests and Talents	258
	3 My Roles in Life	260
	4 My Core Values	262
	5 My Strengths and Weaknesses	264
	6 My Support Team	266
	7 My Personal Mission Statement	268
My Masterplan		271
Epilogue		275
Resources		277

FOREWORD

I first met Gay Page when she was sitting in one of my classes. Instantly she was lighting up the room with her bright smile and joyous wisdom. People wanted some of what she had. Her spiritual clarity made it clear she could be teaching with the light she exuded. When Gay spoke, people listened.

It wasn't long before Gay was enticing all of us in the classroom with chapters from her new book that she was in the process of creating. It was apparent *The Shift Code: Your Personal Empowerment Masterplan* wasn't meant to just be read. The beauty of this book is its gift of practicality for daily implementation. It is beautifully crafted with thought-provoking ideas and exercises that make it a personal journey in self-awareness and growth. The daily routine of positive affirmations, self-exploration exercises, and journaling will give you the path to making the shift in your life you desire.

You are one-in-a-million-billion-trillion! You are one in infinity. Through your journey in *The Shift Code,* you will reveal how special and precious you are. You are necessary to the Universe for it to be complete, not in an egotistical way, but in a sense that shows you that you belong, that you are important, and that you matter—just like every other unique one-in-a-million being.

What would it be like if you treated yourself that way? What if you treated others that way? Imagine a world full of people who treated everyone that way! *The Shift Code* explores ideas, virtues, and values designed to inspire living from the essence of greatness that resides in your soul—guided by the infinite spirit of love connecting everyone and everything on earth.

I always felt Gay's desire to have the people around her live a life of ever expanding good. She wants you to be the master of your shift so you too can live a happy and abundant life. Her code for shifting has been successfully used by people of all ages—from parents introducing virtues and values to their children, to college students setting their path in life, to adults for personal development. In this book, Gay gives you the tools to move from where you are to making your heart's dreams come true. You will expand your awareness and change your life.

Rev. Christian Sorensen, D. D.

PREFACE

I am writing this book to share my recipe for living an abundant, happy, and successful life. My goal is to help you become the "master of your shift" and lead the life of your dreams.

I have practiced the techniques I'll share with you for over thirty-five years and they work. By following this daily routine, I have cultivated an optimistic perspective on life and ingrained habits that help me be resilient when confronted with unexpected challenges and negative experiences. My natural state is to wake up smiling and go to sleep with a deep sense of peace. I feel exuberance deep within my soul and live by spiritual principles that guide my life with grace and gratitude.

My techniques have evolved through study, observation, experimentation, and practice. Although they're not difficult, they do require determination and commitment. Becoming the "master of your shift" doesn't happen overnight, it's a lifelong pursuit and practice.

If I miss one day of practice, I notice it.
If I miss two days of practice, the critics notice it.
If I miss three days of practice, the audience notices it.
– Ignacy Jan Paderewski

The good news is that anyone can make changes at any age or stage in life and every human can choose to live an exuberant life. The key to tapping into your inner joy and happiness is being committed to learning and practicing techniques to rewire your thoughts to create better habits.

Think of it this way, your brain is prewired with neural pathways that support your basic bodily functions. You don't have to tell yourself how to breathe; the neural pathways tell your body to do it automatically. Throughout childhood, you built new neural pathways that instilled important life skills like learning how to walk and brushing your teeth. Unfortunately, along the way you may have also created some neural pathways that instilled habits or behaviors that may be holding you back today.

The techniques I'm sharing with you are my personal success plan. If you practice them, they will help you create new thoughts, which create new neural pathways and habits so you can live the life of your dreams. Your journey begins today.

If you don't like the road you're walking, start paving another one!
– Dolly Parton

INTRODUCTION

Life is all about choices and you have made the choice to unleash your inner fire and achieve your dreams by changing your thinking, so let's get started. The concept is simple; change your thinking, change your life. However, putting that into action and building new thought patterns and habits takes perseverance and time.

This 105-day/15-week action plan is designed to support your quest for living your best life. It will help you rewire your thoughts to create new neural pathways in your brain, which in turn create new habits for lasting positive change. Why 105 days over 15 weeks? Because medical experts estimate that it can take 10,000 repetitions practiced over a period of about three months to create a new neural pathway and new behavior.

Yikes! That sounds like a lot of practice, and it is, but you're not alone on your journey. By following the steps and exercises outlined in this plan you'll soon be able to see and feel changes in your outlook on life and celebrate the success that comes with your new perspective.

The key to mastering your shift is practicing the daily routine and building your self-awareness. Think of the number of years of daily practice that premiere athletes like Tiger Woods, Michael Jordan, and Serena Willams put in to achieve success in their sports. Musicians, dancers, artists, actors, computer wizards, business executives, race car drivers, and experts in all fields take years to hone their skills. To build your new neural pathways and better habits for lasting change in your life, you need that same commitment.

You might be thinking that these athletes and successful people have something you don't, and that isn't true. All human beings have neural pathways created by ingrained thought patterns. Just as Tiger's, Michael's, and Serena's thoughts created their neural pathways and skills, your thoughts have created the pathways that have determined the road you're currently following in life. This plan will help you create a new roadmap and system of superhighways to help you achieve your dreams.

Another way of thinking about this is that thoughts become things, and if you're putting negative thoughts into the energy flowing through the universe, then the universe simply responds by returning negativity into your life. The universe honors your thoughts as you believe them. The good news is that you can choose your thoughts and let go of negativity to feel better and be happier.

People are just as happy as they make their minds up to be.
– Abraham Lincoln

Although my intention for sharing this plan is to help you rewire your thoughts to empower you to live a more enriched life, your personal masterplan may have a more specific intention, such as creating wealth, losing weight, getting in shape, learning a skill to improve your career options, or expanding your circle of friends. If you would like to set a specific intention, please complete the following sentence. My intention for this 105-day/15-week journey is to (_fill in the blank_).

Here's the awesome-sauce in this program—once you instill the habits of the daily routine and complete your journey, you can reset and do it again and again for new intentions, bigger dreams, and continued growth throughout your life. I live an abundant life and am more content and happier than ever because I still practice this daily routine.

DAILY ROUTINE

Great news! This routine primarily revolves around developing optimistic self-talk and can be practiced anytime, anywhere. Rewiring your self-talk from negative to positive is a key part of changing your thoughts and behaviors. First, you need to become aware of the self-talk of what I call your "chatter brain" generates. Years ago, before I started using this daily routine, my chatter brain would prattle on and on all day about insignificant things. It would judge me, my actions, friends, family, and strangers—it primarily dwelled in unhelpful negativity. However, once I understood that I could consciously change the thoughts in my chatter brain, I began feeding it positive thoughts to repeat rather than letting it feed in the pond scum of judgmental unconsciousness.

KEYS TO SUCCESS

1) Practice, Practice, Practice! Commit to completing the steps in the routine every day. Only through consistency of repetition over time will you create the new neural pathways and behaviors vital to helping you change your habits and realize your dreams.

2) Take Action! You can dream about whatever it is you desire and ask the universe to give it to you, but without taking the steps necessary to achieve your intended outcome, it will always remain a dream. If Tiger, Michael, and Serena only dreamed of success and never practiced the skills of their respective sports, they would never have risen to the top of their games and we wouldn't know their names today.

3) Do Not Stop! Try, try, again. If you miss an item in the daily routine or skip a day of practice, don't give up. Every day gives you a new opportunity to continue your journey.

4) Adopt the mantra, "I'm the master of my shift!" Whenever you notice your chatter brain going bonkers with negative, judgmental, or otherwise bad thoughts, tell it to "Stop!" Replace it with a positive thought and pat yourself on the back for awakening your consciousness.

PRACTICING THE ROUTINE

MORNING
- When you wake up, smile, and say, "I am grateful for this day and the positive shift I'm creating in my life!"
- Read the daily action plan in your workbook. Make note of any additional affirmations or self-talk you want to incorporate throughout the day.
- Identify one or more action steps you can initiate toward your intention today.

THROUGHOUT THE DAY
- Repeat the daily affirmation and any additional affirmations you have written or positive self-talk you created to reprogram your chatter brain.
- Reflect on what the mindful brain fuel (topic of the day), quote of the day, and self-reflection question(s) mean to you.
- Exercise. This can be anything from walking the dog to working out at the gym, but it is extremely important to get your body moving every day. While you exercise, repeat your affirmations, envision your future, and *embody the feelings* of having already achieved your intention.

EVENING
- Review the daily plan checklist and check off the items you completed.
- Answer the self-reflection question, and jot down any additional thoughts or feelings about your journey.
- When you go to bed, close your eyes, smile, and say, "I am grateful for this day and appreciate the positive shift I created in my life today!"

BONUS ACTIVITIES

There are many activities that can supercharge the activation of shift in your life. Here are a few you can add to your daily routine:
- Meditate.
- Engage in a random act of kindness.
- Pay it forward.
- Read an inspirational book.
- Experience AWE! Take a moment to soak in the beauty of Mother Nature. Notice a beautiful flower, a tree, the ocean, or a mountain—take a breath and hold that picture in your *mind* (not your cell phone).

DAILY GUIDE AND WORKBOOK

SECTIONS

Week | Day	Each week you'll explore a new theme and every day a different topic related to the theme.
Mindful Brain Fuel	This is food for thought about the topic of the day.
Affirmation	Each day you will have an affirmation to stimulate your positive self-talk. As you become more comfortable with consciously directing your self-talk, I encourage you to add your own affirmations directed at your personal intention.
Checklist	Review the checklist every morning to activate your positive self-talk and remind yourself of what you need to accomplish during the day. Then in the evening check off the items you completed. This will help with consistency and practice, as well as help you track your progress.
Unveiling Your True Self	This is your space for self-reflection. Write down your feelings or anything personal you want to remember about your journey. I suggest you read the question in the morning, think about it during the day, and then write your answer in the evening.
Quote	There will be a new inspirational quote every day that is related to the topic of the day. The intent is to further inspire you.

NOTE

You may find that you need more than one day to think about your views on some of the topics. I urge you to take all the time you need—even if that means it takes multiple days on the same topic.

WEEK 1

WHO AM I?

The Shift Code Daily Routine Checklist

WEEK ONE | *Who Am I?*	Day 1	Day 2	Day 3	Day 4	Day 5	Day 6	Day 7
In the Morning:							
I began my day by smiling and saying, "I am grateful for this day and the positive shift I'm creating in my life!"							
I read the daily action plan in my workbook.							
I made note of the focus of my affirmation(s) and self-talk for the day.							
I identified one or more action steps for the day.							
During the Day:							
I repeated my affirmation(s) and consciously reprogrammed my chatter brain's self-talk.							
I reflected on the Mindful Brain Fuel daily inspiration and quote of the day.							
I initiated my action step(s) for today.							
I exercised.							
In the Evening:							
I checked off the items I completed on the daily plan.							
I answered the self-reflection question.							
I jotted down my thoughts about my journey.							
I ended my day by smiling and saying, "I am grateful for this day and the positive shift I created in my life today!"							
Bonus Activities:							
I meditated.							
I completed a random act of kindness.							
I paid it forward.							
I read an inspirational book.							
I experienced AWE!							
Other: _____							

WEEK ONE

Who Am I?

DAY 1

My Dream . . .

DREAMING BIG is awesome! It's all about possibilities and potential. It's the free spirit within you that has no limitations. Close your eyes and feel it! Open your eyes and see yourself celebrating with family and friends when you reach your dream. Feel the excitement of pure joy and adrenaline coursing through every cell in your body.

Wait! What if you fail? It can be scary to DREAM BIG because fear of failure can creep into the picture. Okay, STOP that thought right now and replace it with the bliss you felt the moment before you read that sentence. The ability to reframe and replace negativity is what this journey will ingrain in you over the next weeks and months. You will feel fear—that's perfectly natural—but it's how you decide to use it that matters. Stay in fear or move forward—it's your choice.

Your life's dream is in your soul just waiting to be released. Finding your dream is more than chasing success or achieving external goals; it's about uncovering the essence of who you are and aligning your actions with your deepest passions and desires. It's a journey of self-discovery and fulfillment that can lead to a life filled with joy, peace, love, and awe.

Your journey begins with finding out who you are. It involves dreaming, introspection, exploration, and the courage to explore your inner being. I encourage you to pursue this adventure with an open heart and mind so you can unleash your authentic self and live a life of purpose, joy, and fulfillment. By practicing the daily routine in this workbook, you will gain a deeper understanding of yourself and ultimately determine who you want to be and how you want to interact with the world.

Each day during your journey, you will reflect on a question to help you awaken your consciousness. It's only through understanding who you are today that you will be able to define who you want to become and how you want to live your life.

Today, reflect on your life's dream and answer the question "If you could do anything in life, knowing you would not fail, what would you do?" Reflect on what it would mean to live this dream—for you, your family, for the world. DREAM BIG! Ideas can always be scaled back, but it's much more difficult to reach higher once you've set a plateau.

I'm the master of my shift!

AFFIRMATION

My dreams result in good flowing to and through everything in my life.

WEEK ONE   **DAY 1**

Unveiling Your True Self

If you could do anything in life, knowing you would not fail, what would you do?

_____

_____

_____

_____

_____

_____

_____

_____

_____

_____

_____

_____

_____

_____

_____

Climb every mountain, Ford every stream,
Follow every rainbow, 'Til you find your dream.
– Richard Rodgers & Oscar Hammerstein

WEEK ONE

Who Am I?

DAY 2

My Interests and Talents

Interest and talent are like cousins—related but not quite the same. Your interests may differ greatly from your innate talents or they may align perfectly. I've known people that love to play the piano but they weren't very good at it. Let's just say, Beethoven wouldn't have been impressed. On the flip side, others were loaded with talent, but not the interest.

Throughout history there have been magical moments where interest and talent have met, shook hands, and created genius—Bach, Mozart, Einstein, da Vinci, Curie, and Hawking to name a few. However, most of us are somewhere in the middle and that's okay! Today, you have the opportunity to take a closer look at what excites you and what you're naturally good at—in other words, identify your interests and talents.

Interests spark your curiosity, grab your attention, and motivate you. They are driven by what you enjoy, what fascinates you, and what lights you up inside. The cool thing about interests is that they can and will probably change over time as you try new things, meet new people, and have new adventures.

Talent, on the other hand, is more about what comes naturally to you. It's often characterized by an innate ability to perform certain tasks exceptionally well with relative ease and proficiency. Talents can encompass a wide range of abilities, including artistic, intellectual, athletic, or interpersonal skills, and while they may be influenced by genetics and innate abilities, they also require nurturing, practice, and development to reach their full potential.

Today, think about what interests capture your imagination and attention, and identify your innate abilities and skills. Don't worry if your interests don't align with all of your talents. The purpose here is to objectively identify what you like and what you're good at. And hey, just like you're learning to rewire that busy chatter in your brain, you can use your talents to cultivate new skills that support your interests.

I'm the master of my shift!

AFFIRMATION

I am grateful for the harmony between my interests and talents, knowing that they empower me to live the life of my dreams.

Week One

Unveiling Your True Self

Day 2

What are your interests?   *What are your talents?*

Go confidently in the direction of your dreams! Live the life you've imagined.
– Henry David Thoreau

WEEK ONE

Who Am I?

DAY 3

My Roles in Life

Defining your roles in life is an essential aspect of your personal development. Today, you will identify all the roles you currently play in life. Example of roles include being a parent, child, brother, sister, cousin, friend, student, teacher, mentor, coach, employer, employee, advocate, leader, follower, caregiver, philanthropist, etc.

1) Using the Defining My Roles template, begin by making a list of the various roles and relationships in your life including family, friendships, workplace, community, and social groups.

2) Think about the specific responsibilities and obligations associated with each person or group on your list and write down any pros or cons regarding your role in that relationship.

3) Then assign a score from 0—10 with 10 being awesome. In considering your score, think about what matters to you most, what you aspire to achieve in different areas of your life, and if your values and priorities align with that role. Your answer to those questions will influence your score and begin to reveal any relationships that may be holding you back or helping you move forward.

Here's the tough part: In reviewing your scores, you'll need to analyze the limits of your involvement and the extent of your commitments within each role. Be realistic about what you can reasonably manage and don't hesitate to say no when necessary. You may need to set stricter boundaries or even end some relationships to focus on your priorities and the intention you set for this journey.

As you're making these decisions, ask for feedback from trusted friends, family members, mentors, or colleagues about how they perceive your roles and contributions. Their insights can provide valuable perspective and help you refine your understanding of your roles.

As you continue to learn and grow throughout your life, realize that roles and relationships are not static and they will change over time. It's important to reassess your roles as your circumstances, priorities, and aspirations evolve, and be open and flexible to adjusting your relationships to maintain your well-being and navigate transitions and challenges more effectively.

I'm the master of my shift!

AFFIRMATION

I embrace the diversity of roles that enrich my life and empower me to grow and thrive each day.

WEEK ONE

DAY 3

Unveiling Your True Self

DEFINE YOUR ROLES

ROLE	PERSON or GROUP	PROS	CONS	SCORE

I alone cannot change the world, but I can cast a stone across the water to create many ripples.
– **Mother Teresa**

WEEK ONE

Who Am I?

DAY 4

My Core Values

Honoring and following your core values will help you navigate precarious situations with grace and ease because they help you focus on choosing a path that aligns with your ethics and personal code of conduct. Adhering to your values will help you live with a higher purpose and avoid falling into detrimental situations that could damage your reputation—or worse.

The following list highlights a few core values. Your values may be among these or you may choose something different, but it's imperative that the values you choose truly represent you. I suggest you adopt three to four values so you can focus on living each value every day. If you choose more than that it can dilute your commitment to embodying the value. It's also important to note that values can change over time, so what is of the highest importance to you today, may not be the same in ten or twenty years.

Accountability
Authenticity
Compassion
Courage
Empathy
Fairness
Generosity
Gratitude
Grace
Honesty
Humility
Integrity
Kindness
Love
Loyalty
Open-mindedness
Perseverance
Resilience
Respect
Responsibility
Self-discipline

I'm the master of my shift!

AFFIRMATION

I affirm my core values as guiding principles that shape my actions and decisions. State your values, (i.e., integrity, compassion, resilience, and authenticity) are the foundation of my character and lead me towards a life of meaning, fulfillment, and alignment with my true self.

WEEK ONE   **DAY 4**

Unveiling Your True Self

What are your core values?

_____
_____
_____
_____
_____
_____
_____
_____
_____
_____
_____
_____
_____
_____
_____

Your beliefs become your thoughts, your thoughts become your words, your words become your actions, your actions become your habits, your habits become your values, your values become your destiny.
– Mahatma Gandhi

WEEK ONE

Who Am I?

DAY 5

My Strengths and Weaknesses

Today, it's all about figuring out your strengths and weaknesses. Why? Because understanding what you're great at and what you could use some help with is like having a secret weapon for personal growth. When you know both sides of yourself, you can totally rock what you're naturally good at and find people who are experts in the areas where you're not. Understand that most of us are way more confident and effective when we're working in our genius zone. You know, the zone where everything just clicks. You feel on top of the world, super productive, and like you can handle anything life throws your way.

Your strengths are basically the keys to unlocking your potential. They allow you to crush your goals, shine in the things you love, and make an impact both at work and in your personal life. Imagine getting to spend more time focusing on what you're naturally good at. Who wouldn't want that?

Now let's talk about weaknesses. Yeah, they're not fun to admit, but accepting that you're not awesome at everything is actually a good thing! It gives you the chance to grow, learn, and even build a little humility. Plus, no one's perfect.

Every single one of us has some weak spots. And guess what? Those weaknesses are gifts that give you opportunities for collaboration. Your not-so-great area might be someone else's jam, which means you get to work together, creating a win-win situation that builds stronger connections and boosts teamwork.

Recognizing where you excel and where you fall short doesn't make you any less capable; it makes you authentic. And authenticity is a superpower in itself. When you own all parts of who you are, people respect you more and you can navigate life with more confidence, support, and success. So, embrace all the good, the bad, and everything in between!

If you're interested in finding out more about your strengths, I suggest reading *StrengthsFinder* 2.0 by Tom Rath. It is accompanied by an online assessment of your strengths and is a great tool for learning more about your strengths and how they interact with others. NOTE: *StrengthsFinder* has been rebranded as *CliftonStrengths*, but it's the same assessment.

I'm the master of my shift!

AFFIRMATION

I embrace both my personal strengths and weaknesses as integral parts of my journey. My strengths empower me to excel and make meaningful contributions, while my weaknesses offer opportunities for growth and learning.

WEEK ONE

Unveiling Your True Self

DAY 5

What are your strengths?   *What are your weaknesses?*

*Most people think they know what they are good at. They are usually wrong...
And yet, a person can perform only from strength.*
– Peter Drucker

WEEK ONE

Who Am I?

DAY 6

My Support Team

We all need people around us that encourage and support our dreams and share our values. Today, you will decide who needs to be on your support team. This is an important component of your journey because you need to surround yourself with people who inspire you and that you respect and trust.

When selecting individuals for your personal support team, it's essential to consider their qualities and how they align with your needs. You need to choose people that you trust, have values that align with yours, and that will be a positive influence. Qualities you should look for in team members include, but are not limited to empathy, understanding, great listening skills, wisdom and experience, positive and supportive attitude, reliability, and trustworthiness.

When you are recruiting team members, you should establish your expectations by clearly identifying their time commitment and parameters of their role on your team. You need to articulate the importance of confidentiality, fostering an environment of trust, respect, open-mindedness, flexibility, open lines of communication, honest feedback, and authenticity.

Caring for your personal support team is an ongoing process. You need to regularly acknowledge and thank your team members and have open and honest conversations with them regarding their role and contributions to your team. Some members may naturally drift away as your needs change, while others may become more integral over time. As you progress, you may need to reassess your team composition and seek out new members who can provide the support you need.

Using the My Support Team template, write down the people you turn to for support.
- Who are they—parent, sibling, relative, friend, teacher, colleague, coach, other?
- How do they help?
- What can you count on them for—advice, a laugh, a place to chill out?
- How would you score their level of support? 0—10 with 10 being 100% supportive.
- Who is missing from this list that needs to be on your team?

I'm the master of my shift!

AFFIRMATION

I have people who care about me, support my dreams, and help me when I need it.

Week One

Unveiling Your True Self

Day 6

MY SUPPORT TEAM

NAME	RELATIONSHIP	HOW TO THEY HELP?	SCORE
EXAMPLE: Marci	My mother	She is my biggest cheerleader and supports my dreams.	10

Surround yourself only with people who are going to lift you higher.
– Oprah Winfrey

WEEK ONE

Who Am I?

DAY 7

My Personal Mission Statement

Personal mission statements can be hard to write! They need to be concise, clear, vivid, and inspiring. Your personal mission statement should be your guiding star and reflect your vision for living a fulfilling and successful life. It should include your purpose (reason for being), your guiding principles (core values), who you are (interests), and what contribution you would like to make during your life.

EXAMPLES OF PERSONAL MISSION STATEMENTS
- My mission in life is not merely to survive, but to thrive, and to do so with some passion, some compassion, some humor, and some style. – Maya Angelou
- To serve the poorest of the poor with love and compassion. – Mother Teresa
- To be the change I wish to see in the world. – Mahatma Gandhi

STEPS TO DEVELOP YOUR PERSONAL MISSION STATEMENT
1) Reflect on Your Values and Beliefs
   - Take time to reflect on what matters most to you. Consider your core values, beliefs, passions, and principles that guide your decisions and actions.
   - Ask yourself questions such as: What brings meaning and fulfillment to my life? What do I stand for? What are my strengths and talents? What impact do I want to make in the world?

2) Define Your Purpose
   - Clarify your purpose or overarching mission in life. What do you want to achieve or contribute during your time on earth? What do you want to accomplish in various areas of your life, i.e., family, relationships, personal growth, professionally, and community involvement?

3) Draft Your Mission Statement
   - Write a rough draft of your mission statement, incorporating your values, beliefs, purpose, and goals you've identified. Keep it concise, clear, and inspiring. It should encapsulate the essence of who you are, what you stand for, and what you're committed to achieving.
   - Review, edit, and refine your statement as needed to ensure it resonates with you on a deep level and accurately reflects your values, beliefs, and goals.

Once you've finalized your mission statement, integrate it into your daily life. Use it as a guiding principle to make decisions, set priorities, and take actions that align with your values and goals. Regularly revisit and reflect on your mission statement to ensure it remains relevant and meaningful to you. Finally, embrace your mission as a source of inspiration, motivation, and purpose, empowering you to live authentically and make a positive impact in the world.

I'm the master of my shift!

AFFIRMATION

I embrace my personal mission statement as a source of inspiration, motivation, and purpose, empowering me to live authentically and make a positive impact in the world.

WEEK ONE — — — — — — — — — — **DAY 7**

Unveiling Your True Self

What is your personal mission in life? My mission in life is to . . .

_____

_____

_____

_____

_____

_____

_____

_____

_____

_____

_____

_____

_____

_____

_____

**You have brains in your head. You have feet in your shoes.
You can steer yourself in any direction you choose.
– Dr. Seuss**

Week 2

Becoming The Master of My Shift!

The Shift Code Daily Routine Checklist

WEEK TWO | *Becoming the Master of My Shift!*	Day 1	Day 2	Day 3	Day 4	Day 5	Day 6	Day 7
In the Morning:							
I began my day by smiling and saying, "I am grateful for this day and the positive shift I'm creating in my life!"							
I read the daily action plan in my workbook.							
I made note of the focus of my affirmation(s) and self-talk for the day.							
I identified one or more action steps for the day.							
During the Day:							
I repeated my affirmation(s) and consciously reprogrammed my chatter brain's self-talk.							
I reflected on the Mindful Brain Fuel daily inspiration and quote of the day.							
I initiated my action step(s) for today.							
I exercised.							
In the Evening:							
I checked off the items I completed on the daily plan.							
I answered the self-reflection question.							
I jotted down my thoughts about my journey.							
I ended my day by smiling and saying, "I am grateful for this day and the positive shift I created in my life today!"							
Bonus Activities:							
I meditated.							
I completed a random act of kindness.							
I paid it forward.							
I read an inspirational book.							
I experienced AWE!							
Other: _____							

WEEK TWO

Becoming the Master of My Shift!

DAY 1

Wake Up!

The first step to making any kind of change is simply becoming aware of your current thought patterns and beliefs. Think of it as hitting the "wake-up" button on your brain. By paying attention to what's running through your mind and how those thoughts are shaping your emotions and actions, you'll start to see how everything's connected. Bottom line: before you can change your thoughts, you've got to wake up to them first!

So, how do you start this process? Enter mindfulness. It's all about being present and really tuning in to your thoughts and feelings without judging them. Mindfulness is like the MVP of personal empowerment and will definitely be a recurring theme as you go on this journey of growth.

As you start paying attention to the chatter in your brain, you'll get a front-row seat to how your mind works. You'll notice those recurring thoughts, the patterns you default to, and even some biases or beliefs that you might want to reframe or ditch altogether. This awareness is key to steering your thoughts in a positive direction.

Your "wake-up call" will also shine a light on your core beliefs—those deeply ingrained ideas we have about ourselves, others, and the world. These beliefs usually start forming when we're young, and they can have a major impact on how we behave and respond emotionally. If you discover that some of these core beliefs are holding you back, now's the perfect time to figure out where they came from, thank them for the lesson (even if it's a weird one), and swap them out for beliefs that align with the future you're working toward.

With this newfound awareness, you're ready to start your journey of intentional change. By questioning those limiting beliefs, adopting healthier thought patterns, and staying mindful, you'll gain deeper insights into yourself. And that's the first step to reshaping your experiences and transforming your life.

I'm the master of my shift!

AFFIRMATION

I am the master of my thoughts! I am aware of my self-talk and replace negative chatter with meaningful positive thoughts.

WEEK TWO — — — — — — — — — — — **DAY 1**

Unveiling Your True Self

What thoughts does your chatter brain regularly dwell on?

*If you want to make your dreams come true,
the first thing you have to do is wake up.*
– J.M. Power

WEEK TWO

Becoming the Master of My Shift!

DAY 2

Identify Negative Patterns

Perpetual negative thoughts can really mess with your mental well-being and lead to things like anxiety, depression, and a serious dip in self-esteem. Negative thoughts can sneak their way into your relationships, your work, and just generally tank your overall quality of life. And, if left unchecked, those repetitive negative patterns can turn into a constant buzz in your brain, leaving you feeling sad, hopeless, and completely drained.

Negative thoughts are like:
- dark clouds hovering over your head, blocking you from seeing how amazing and capable you really are;
- shadows that block out the light and suck the color out of your world;
- a tangled mess of weeds, suffocating your soul and choking out every bit of positivity and good vibes you've got;
- a broken record on repeat, drowning out any possibility of upbeat, happy thoughts;
- an endless cycle of self-doubt and worry that leaves you stuck in a loop of "what-if's" and "I cant's";
- a constant chatter that tears you down, fills you with criticism and makes you feel defeated..

Negative thoughts can be pretty gross and overwhelming, making it hard to focus on anything but the negativity. YUCK! Who wants that kind of garbage swirling around in their brain? Not me! And I'm betting you're not exactly signing up for it either.

Today, take a little time to pinpoint any of those negative or unhelpful thought patterns that are contributing to your stress, anxiety, or just making life less fun. If you come across thoughts that aren't helping you live your best, most joyful life, it's time to kick them to the curb and start shifting your mindset in a more positive direction.

I'm the master of my shift!

AFFIRMATION

I am the master of my thoughts! I consciously focus my chatter brain on thoughts that positively influence my life.

WEEK TWO — — — — — — — — — — — **DAY 2**

Unveiling Your True Self

How are your chatter brain thoughts influencing your life?

_____
_____
_____
_____
_____
_____
_____
_____
_____
_____
_____
_____
_____

Within your own mentality there lies a source of energy stronger than electricity, more potent than high explosives, unlimited and inexhaustible. You only need to make conscious contact with it to set it working in your affairs.
– Emmet Fox

WEEK TWO

Becoming the Master of My Shift!

DAY 3

Challenge Negative Thoughts

Negative thoughts are sneaky little things creeping into our minds like shadows and quietly shifting how we see the world. They have a way of messing with our emotions and actions, stirring up self-doubt, making the future seem pretty bleak, or even turning every small worry into a full-blown catastrophe. But here's the good news: by confronting these thoughts head-on, we can totally transform them, take control of that chatter brain, and start living a more fulfilling life.

Yesterday, you began to notice your negative thought patterns. Today, it's time to take it a step further by challenging and questioning their truth in what you're thinking. You are now a neutral observer, stepping back from your thoughts and looking at them without reacting. Recognize them for what they are—just patterns of thinking. Some of these thoughts might not even be based in reality or they could be old ideas that no longer mean anything to you.

Start by identifying one negative thought, then ask yourself:
- Is this thought based on fact, or am I making it up?
- Am I jumping to conclusions here?
- Is this thought holding me back from living my best life?
- Is this thought helpful? If not, it's time to reframe and swap it out for something better!

As you go through this process of becoming aware of and challenging your negative thoughts, remember you're not alone. Everyone deals with self-doubt and negativity from time to time. Be sure to treat yourself with the same kindness and understanding that you'd show to a good friend who's going through a tough time. You deserve that!

** If you are having difficulty with persistent negative thoughts, don't hesitate to reach out to friends, family, or mental health professionals for support. Talking about your negative thoughts with others can provide perspective, support, and reassurance.

I'm the master of my shift!

AFFIRMATION

I am the master of my self-talk and I choose to think optimistic positive thoughts!

WEEK TWO — DAY 3

Unveiling Your True Self

Are any of your negative thoughts based in fact? Identify the benefits of reinterpreting the thought or situation from an unbiased, nonreactive perspective.

Don't be afraid to shift or pivot.
— Alex Rodriguez

WEEK TWO
Becoming the Master of My Shift!

DAY 4
Reframe Negative Thoughts

Reframing negative thoughts isn't some magic, quick-fix solution. It's a skill you've got to build over time with practice, patience, and a good dose of self-awareness. Once you get the hang of it, you'll be able to break free from the grip of negativity and embrace a more positive, resilient outlook. Since our perception or how we see the world shapes our reality, why not choose to see the glass half-full and create a mindset that helps you thrive and tackle whatever life throws your way?

When you reframe negative thoughts, you're not just being more optimistic, you're also building resilience and learning how to handle adversity and life's challenges. The only way to break free from those old thought patterns and create a more positive mindset is to practice swapping out that negative chatter for some good old-fashioned positive self-talk.

EXAMPLES OF REFRAMING

- I'm a failure.
+ Every failure is a chance for me to grow and learn. Mistakes are just stepping stones on my way to success, and I handle them with resilience and determination.

- I'm terrible at public speaking. I always mess up and embarrass myself.
+ Public speaking is a skill I'm still working on. Every time I do it, I get a little better and a little more confident.

- I'll never be able to lose weight. I've tried everything and nothing works.
+ Losing weight is a journey that requires patience and persistence. Every step I take towards better nutrition and regular exercise brings me closer to my goals.

- I'll never find someone who truly loves and accepts me for who I am.
+ I trust that the right person is out there, someone who appreciates me for who I am and shares my values.

I'm the master of my shift!

AFFIRMATION

I am the master of my thoughts and I choose to be a positive thinker.

WEEK TWO — — — — — — — — — — **DAY 4**

Unveiling Your True Self

List the negative thoughts you have and reframe them from a positive perspective.

_____
_____
_____
_____
_____
_____
_____
_____
_____
_____
_____
_____
_____
_____
_____
_____

If my mind can conceive it, if my heart can believe it, then I can achieve it.
– Muhammad Ali

WEEK TWO

Becoming the Master of My Shift!

DAY 5

Mindfulness

Today I'm introducing the concept of mindfulness and we'll explore it further in Week Four. Mindfulness is about being fully present in the moment, intentionally paying attention to what's going on around you—and within you—without any judgment. It's a practice of tuning in to your thoughts, feelings, bodily sensations, and your environment, with a sense of openness and curiosity. When you embrace mindfulness, you create space for clarity, calmness, and a deeper connection to yourself and the world around you.

A lot of people practice mindfulness through meditation, which is awesome. I encourage you to take it even further and make it a part of your daily life—weave it into everything you do. By adopting mindfulness as a way of being, you can transform your own life as well as the lives of those you interact with. Trust me, it's worth it.

For me, approaching life mindfully has helped me show up more fully in each moment, especially with the people I care about most.

Over time, my mindfulness practice has made me more self-aware, more compassionate, and more forgiving. It's helped me bounce back from tough situations with more resilience and find a sense of inner peace and happiness that radiates from deep within my soul, allowing me to move through life with more grace and ease.

Throughout this journey, we'll explore different mindfulness techniques like meditation. But for now, just start by being more aware of your thoughts and how they shape your reactions in the moment. For example, when someone cuts you off in traffic, instead of going straight to frustration, try this: take a deep breath, let it go, and be grateful no one got hurt. Notice how the tension lifts when you choose to release it. The truth is, you can't change what just happened, but you can choose how you respond to it.

Remember, you are the master of your shift!

I'm the master of my shift!

AFFIRMATION

I am the master of my thoughts and can stop negative thoughts in the moment and replace them with positive self-talk.

WEEK TWO — — — — — — — — — — — **DAY 5**

Unveiling Your True Self

Present Moment Awareness—What are you experiencing right now, in this moment? What thoughts are passing through your mind? How does your body feel physically? Can you identify any sensations or tensions? What emotions are you experiencing, and how are they manifesting in your body?

_____
_____
_____
_____
_____
_____
_____
_____
_____
_____
_____
_____
_____
_____
_____

You do not find the happy life. You make it.
– Camilla Eyring Kimball

WEEK TWO

Becoming the Master of My Shift!

DAY 6

Activate and Engage

Living a successful and joyful life is all about how we engage with it. One of the most powerful tools we have at our disposal is positive self-talk. The way we speak to ourselves matters. By consciously choosing to focus on empowering, uplifting thoughts, we can transform how we see challenges, setbacks, and opportunities. Positive self-talk boosts our confidence, helps us manage stress, and pushes us to keep going, even when things get tough. So, next time you catch yourself thinking "I can't do this," flip the script to "I've got this!" You'll be surprised how much of a difference it makes.

But here's the thing: while your mind is getting all that positive reinforcement, your body needs a little love too. This is where exercise comes in. Moving your body is one of the best ways to activate those feel-good endorphins and release any pent-up tension. Whether it's hitting the gym, going for a walk, dancing in your living room, or even trying a new yoga class, exercise not only boosts your physical health but also sharpens your mental focus and lifts your mood.

It's like a double win for your mind and body. Plus, it doesn't have to be complicated—just get moving in whatever way feels good to you.

Let's not forget about hobbies. Having something you love to do outside of your daily grind is essential for joy and fulfillment. Whether it's painting, gardening, playing a musical instrument, or even collecting funky socks, hobbies bring a sense of accomplishment and happiness. They give you a break from the pressures of life and remind you that joy is found in the little things. Plus, hobbies can connect us with others who share similar interests, creating a sense of community.

When you combine positive self-talk, regular exercise, and time spent on your favorite hobbies, you're engaging in life in a way that sets you up for success and joy. It's all about creating a balance that makes you feel empowered, energized, and fulfilled.

I'm the master of my shift!

AFFIRMATION

My hobbies and activities activate and engage my thoughts on happiness and joy.

WEEK TWO — — — — — — — — **DAY 6**

Unveiling Your True Self

What hobbies or activities do you currently engage in that bring you joy? What new activities would you like to try?

_____
_____
_____
_____
_____
_____
_____
_____
_____
_____
_____
_____
_____
_____
_____

Happiness is not something ready-made. It comes from your own actions.
– Dalai Lama

WEEK TWO

Becoming the Master of My Shift!

DAY 7

Consistency and Persistence

As previously discussed, changing your thoughts to build new neural pathways and better habits takes time and repetition. You need to be patient and surround yourself with supportive and optimistic people who uplift and inspire you. Their positive energy can help you counteract negativity and reinforce your commitment to your new daily routine. But ultimately it comes down to you being persistent and consistently practicing the elements presented in the daily routine—it always comes down to your choice and dedication.

Persistence will drive you to reach your dreams by cultivating your resilience and ability to bounce back from failure or rejection. Persistence will help you overcome adversity by giving you the will to move forward despite facing obstacles or challenges. It's the relentless determination to persevere and is fueled by your innate spirit, passion, and purpose.

Consistency is you showing up every day regardless of circumstances or internal doubts. It's the commitment to hold yourself accountable for practicing the routine every day. When you're consistent, you develop discipline, self-control, and willpower, which ultimately help you master the skill of positive thinking and live an exuberant life filled with love, joy, peace, and success.

Consistency and persistence are essential to completing your journey—together they will support and guide you. Celebrate them and every small win you have along the way.

I'm the master of my shift!

AFFIRMATION

I feel joy and excitement tingling throughout my body as I celebrate my consistent practice of reprogramming my self-talk and etching the components of the daily routine into my life.

WEEK TWO — — — — — — — — — — **DAY 7**

Unveiling Your True Self

What is your plan for being persistent and maintaining consistency as you progress through this journey?

_____
_____
_____
_____
_____
_____
_____
_____
_____
_____
_____
_____
_____
_____

Success is the sum of small efforts, repeated day in and day out.
– Robert Collier

WEEK 3

THE ORCHARD IN YOUR MIND

The Shift Code Daily Routine Checklist

WEEK THREE | *The Orchard in Your Mind*	Day 1	Day 2	Day 3	Day 4	Day 5	Day 6	Day 7
In the Morning:							
I began my day by smiling and saying, "I am grateful for this day and the positive shift I'm creating in my life!"							
I read the daily action plan in my workbook.							
I made note of the focus of my affirmation(s) and self-talk for the day.							
I identified one or more action steps for the day.							
During the Day:							
I repeated my affirmation(s) and consciously reprogrammed my chatter brain's self-talk.							
I reflected on the Mindful Brain Fuel daily inspiration and quote of the day.							
I initiated my action step(s) for today.							
I exercised.							
In the Evening:							
I checked off the items I completed on the daily plan.							
I answered the self-reflection question.							
I jotted down my thoughts about my journey.							
I ended my day by smiling and saying, "I am grateful for this day and the positive shift I created in my life today!"							
Bonus Activities:							
I meditated.							
I completed a random act of kindness.							
I paid it forward.							
I read an inspirational book.							
I experienced AWE!							
Other: _____							

WEEK THREE

DAY 1

The Orchard in Your Mind

Plan

This week focuses on planning, planting, and harvesting the orchard of thoughts in your mind—thoughts that will nourish your soul and support your dreams. Imagine this: You're standing in your backyard surveying the garden beds that you've neglected for far too long. The vegetables are rotting and once vibrant flowers are wilting, overshadowed by the invasive tangled web of weeds that have taken over due to your neglect. In this vision, the tangled web of weeds represents the chaos of thoughts rattling around unconsciously in your chatter brain. How long have those thoughts been plaguing you? Isn't it time to start planning a new garden of positive uplifting thoughts?

As you reflect on the sorry state of your garden, a flicker of determination sparks within you erasing negativity and self-doubt. You decide to roll up your sleeves and restore beauty to your backyard oasis, which activates your superpower of conscious thought to weed out the negative thoughts running through your chatter brain. With a smile on your face and renewed passion in your heart, you begin planning the new orchard in your mind.

Why plan? As Yogi Berra said, "If you don't know where you are going, you might wind up someplace else." Every journey involves some level of planning. For instance, a trip to the grocery store is simple and only involves planning which streets to take, while planning a trip around the world is much more complex and requires strategy, foresight, and in-depth preparation. Planning the garden of thoughts that you want to flourish in your mind is like planning that trip around the world and is critically important in your quest for empowerment, optimism, and contentment.

As you're developing the blueprint for the new thoughts you want to cultivate, consider what areas in your life need attention. Your core values, self-esteem, confidence, happiness, health, fitness, career, or relationships are just a few areas you may want to work on. By carefully planning your orchard around your priorities, you create specific thoughts to encourage, enlighten, and enrich them.

I'm the master of my shift!

AFFIRMATION

I am in charge of my plan for living a happy and fulfilled life.

WEEK THREE — — — — — — — — — — — **DAY 1**

Unveiling Your True Self

What are your priority areas for creating positive thoughts?

_____
_____
_____
_____
_____
_____
_____
_____
_____
_____
_____
_____
_____
_____

If you fail to plan, you're planning to fail.
– Benjamin Franklin

WEEK THREE

The Orchard in Your Mind

DAY 2

Prepare the Soil

The orchard in your mind is more than just a metaphor. It's a reflection of the thoughts and actions you want to develop. Today you will set the stage for your orchard masterpiece by preparing the soil and letting your imagination run wild.

Close your eyes and envision your mind as a vast expanse of fertile soil ready to be cultivated with intention and care. In one section, you see lush beds of vibrant flowers swaying gently in the breeze, the result of sowing seeds of positivity. Another section is neat rows of vegetables thriving under the golden sun representing knowledge and growth. Beyond the flowers and vegetables is an orchard of luscious fruit trees as far as your eyes can see, sprouting wisdom, strength, and resilience.

By meticulously planning each section of your mental garden and properly preparing the soil, you will ensure there is harmony and balance in the variety of thoughts you want to nourish and the new neural pathways you want to create. Although tending to this garden will require dedication and mindfulness, the rewards you reap will be worth your time and effort.

I'm the master of my shift!

AFFIRMATION

My mind is a pristine sanctuary of positive thoughts that nourish my soul and guide my life.

WEEK THREE

DAY 2

Unveiling Your True Self

What will your life look like when your new thoughts grow and bloom with positivity and happiness?

_____

_____

_____

_____

_____

_____

_____

_____

_____

_____

_____

_____

_____

_____

_____

*All you need is the plan, the road map,
and the courage to press on to your destination.*
– Earl Nightingale

WEEK THREE

The Orchard in Your Mind

DAY 3

Plant the Seeds

Today, you have the opportunity to revisit who you are and start prioritizing the thoughts you want to imprint as the baseline self-talk in your chatter brain. These thoughts will come from the categories presented in week one—your dream, core values, roles, strengths and weaknesses, interests and talents, support team, and personal mission statement. Reflect on the components you identified in each of those categories and put them in priority order. Once you have identified your highest priorities, envision the future you want in each one so you can develop and plant the thought seeds needed to realize your desired outcome.

Each category can have many thoughts or affirmations associated with it but for now I suggest writing one overarching statement that embodies the most important thought or belief you want to address. Then choose one category to focus on so you can be hyper-focused on the change you want to create. Choosing more than one category will be overwhelming and create a chaos of self-talk rather than clear, concise, and purposeful thoughts.

Yesterday, you took time to clear out your mind to prepare it for new positive thoughts, and we don't want to clutter it with too much information today. Clutter = bad Feng Shui! As you progress and achieve success by embodying your new thoughts, you can refine them over time to help you keep moving forward and adjusting to your life's journey.

Here are three examples.

Category	Core Values
Affirmation	I live each day honoring my values and principles in every thought, word, and action.

Category	Roles
Affirmation	I embrace my relationships and am grateful for the experiences they bring into my life.

Category	Weaknesses
Affirmation	I am blessed to have people show up in my life that can support and enlighten me.

I'm the master of my shift!

AFFIRMATION

I carefully select and plant thoughts that represent my essence and bloom into my guiding lights.

WEEK THREE   **DAY 3**

Unveiling Your True Self

Write down the names of the seeds (thoughts) you need to plant in your mind today, i.e., joy, exuberance, optimism, financial freedom, integrity, empathy.

_____

_____

_____

_____

_____

_____

_____

_____

_____

_____

_____

_____

_____

_____

_____

Always do your best. What you plant now, you will harvest later.
– Og Mandino

WEEK THREE

DAY 4

The Orchard in Your Mind

Feed

Now that you've identified your priority areas for changing your thoughts, it's time to make sure you feed and water them regularly to ensure they get the necessary nutrients to bloom and flourish. Feeding and watering equates to practice, practice, practice. And the practice of consciously transforming your thoughts requires a heightened awareness of your chatter brain self-talk. Left untended, chatter brain monologues can wander away from nurturing thoughts and fill the void with doubts and fears. This kind of self-talk is unproductive and certainly doesn't help create a mental environment conducive to growth and transformation. Now is the time to double down on raising your level of consciousness throughout the day to bring your chatter brain self-talk back to the nourishing thoughts you planted yesterday.

The keys to success are being persistent and consistent as you become more mindful of your self-talk. Just as a garden can't thrive without care, self-talk can't undergo meaningful transformation without conscious awareness.

By continually practicing making a conscious effort to redirect your thoughts toward your identified priority areas, you build and reinforce the neural pathways associated with these new patterns of thinking.

It's also important to surround yourself with supportive and like-minded people that can bolster your efforts. Engaging in conversations that align with your desired intentions can be enlightening and inspirational and provide encouragement to help keep you motivated. The more you align yourself with people you trust, admire, and would like to emulate, the more nourishment you'll have to nurture and cultivate a mindset capable of blooming into the fullest expression of your potential.

I'm the master of my shift!

AFFIRMATION

I nourish my mind with healthy thoughts and my soul with love and joy.

WEEK THREE

DAY 4

Unveiling Your True Self

How are you caring for yourself and who are you interacting with to ensure you're successful in raising your consciousness to reach your desired intentions?

_____
_____
_____
_____
_____
_____
_____
_____
_____
_____
_____
_____
_____
_____
_____

Sow a thought, and you reap an act. Sow an act, and you reap a habit. Sow a habit, and you reap a character. Sow a character, and you reap a destiny.
– Charles Reade

WEEK THREE

The Orchard in Your Mind

DAY 5

Observe

Today gives you the opportunity to embrace the role of observation. This concept is related to mindfulness and allows you to step back, tune into your inner awareness, and look at the chaos of your own thoughts, emotions, and actions with curiosity, empathy, and openness. Becoming an impartial observer and perceiving your thoughts and actions objectively can be a gateway to understanding, growth, and profound self-awareness.

In relation to the orchard in your mind, observation gives you the ability to stand in awe of the changes being initiated by the positive self-talk blossoming through your careful planning, planting, and feeding this week. You can compare your old chatter brain thoughts with your new consciously driven self-talk and celebrate your increased ability to transcend the perceived limitations of the old chatter.

Observation encourages a heightened state of awareness that fosters gratitude, wonder, and an appreciation for the natural beauty throughout the world.

It cultivates a mindset of being in the present moment without judgment, bias, or reactive emotions and behaviors. Observing is a deliberate choice to engage with curiosity, compassion, and clarity by facilitating self-reflection and introspection. The art of observation lays the foundation for personal growth and transformation, empowering us to identify areas for improvement and make conscious choices aligned with our highest aspirations.

By stepping outside ourselves and discerning the dynamics at play in various situations, we develop a deeper understanding of the motivations, emotions, and intentions driving the actions of others. This builds our emotional intelligence and fosters empathy, compassion, and the ability to navigate interpersonal relationships with grace and understanding. Observers see a world of infinite possibilities where every moment becomes an opportunity for growth, insight, and transformation.

I'm the master of my shift!

AFFIRMATION

I celebrate my observations as opportunities to become more self-aware and improve my emotional intelligence.

WEEK THREE

DAY 5

Unveiling Your True Self

Present Moment Awareness—What are you experiencing right now, in this moment? What thoughts are passing through your mind? How does your body feel physically? Can you identify any sensations or tensions? What emotions are you experiencing, and how are they manifesting in your body?

In the garden of life, have faith in the seeds you've planted. Even when you can't see them sprouting, trust that they are taking root beneath the surface, ready to bloom in due time.
– **Anonymous**

WEEK THREE

The Orchard in Your Mind

DAY 6

Tend and Weed

Why weed? Simply put, you will feel better physically and mentally. Removing irrational negative influences like toxic relationships, pessimistic attitudes, self-defeating beliefs, fear of failure, conflict, and negative internal dialogue creates space for optimism, resilience, confidence, motivation, empowerment, new opportunities, and abundance far beyond the scope of your current imagination.

Let's revisit the orchard in your mind. How does it look? Are any negative thoughts popping up? If so, it's time for some weeding, so grab your gardening gloves, tear out those weeds and refocus your inner dialogue in a positive direction. Be sure to celebrate every negative thought you uproot as a victory in consciously reclaiming your chatter brain's self-talk. I recommend that you physically pat yourself on the back and look in the mirror and tell yourself you did a great job!

The roots of negativity grow deep and take form as prickly thorns and creeping vines. They will fight back and try to cling to your unconscious self. You need to be relentless in your weeding practice. Ultimately as the weeds are cast aside, their darkness will be replaced with a lightness in your spirit and a newfound sense of clarity. Remember, you are stronger than you think! Give yourself some encouragement, stay optimistic, and weed, weed, weed, weed so you can keep positivity and happiness growing and blooming.

I'm the master of my shift!

AFFIRMATION

My self-talk is focused on positive optimistic thoughts that empower me to fulfill my dreams.

WEEK THREE

DAY 6

Unveiling Your True Self

What are three specific thoughts you are permanently removing from your garden?

_____
_____
_____
_____
_____
_____
_____
_____
_____
_____
_____
_____
_____
_____
_____

To have a flourishing garden, you must tend and weed it with care.
Similarly, to have a peaceful and positive mind,
you must tend to your thoughts with mindfulness.
– Anonymous

WEEK THREE

The Orchard in Your Mind

DAY 7

Celebrate the Feast!

As the 70's rock band Three Dog Night said, "Celebrate, celebrate, dance to the music!" To me, that's the perfect way to get up and get moving to celebrate your accomplishments as you progress along this journey. You need to stand in awe of what you're accomplishing and enjoy the beautiful self-talk that you are nurturing in the orchard of your mind. Since thoughts become things and you're growing optimistic positive thoughts, you deserve to celebrate all the great things those thoughts are producing throughout your life.

Imagine your party is in full swing, colorful streamers hang from the ceiling and the sound of laughter fills the room. The DJ is playing your favorite tunes that has everyone on their feet, moving to the beat. As the music pumps through the speakers, the energy in the room intensifies, drawing people closer together in a shared moment of pure joy and celebration. Smiles mirror your happiness as everyone revels in your success.

While you won't always celebrate with a big party, it's important to keep in mind that even small victories can and should be celebrated. Why? Because celebrating success is a powerful motivator and can inspire you to dream bigger and achieve more. It reinforces the positive thoughts, behaviors, and habits you're in the process of creating, and it strengthens your commitment to continuing your quest for personal and professional growth. Celebrations serve as milestones along your journey, marking your accomplishments and providing momentum to propel you forward.

Celebrating success:
- promotes gratitude by allowing you to acknowledge and express appreciation for the support and contributions of others;
- cultivates resilience, which helps you navigate setbacks and challenges more effectively and persevere through difficult times;
- fosters connectedness by bringing people together, strengthening relationships, and building community; and
- helps maintain a healthy work-life balance by providing moments of joy, relaxation, and rejuvenation.

I'm the master of my shift!

AFFIRMATION

When I celebrate my wins, I feel joy and excitement tingling throughout my body.

WEEK THREE   **DAY 7**

Unveiling Your True Self

What is your plan for celebrating success in life—especially the small wins that happen every day as you progress through this personal success journey?

_____
_____
_____
_____
_____
_____
_____
_____
_____
_____
_____
_____
_____
_____
_____

Take time to celebrate your achievements throughout your journey. Be grateful for everything you have accomplished and look forward to what's next.
– Anonymous

WEEK 4

MINDFULNESS

The Shift Code Daily Routine Checklist

WEEK FOUR | *Mindfulness*	Day 1	Day 2	Day 3	Day 4	Day 5	Day 6	Day 7
In the Morning:							
I began my day by smiling and saying, "I am grateful for this day and the positive shift I'm creating in my life!"							
I read the daily action plan in my workbook.							
I made note of the focus of my affirmation(s) and self-talk for the day.							
I identified one or more action steps for the day.							
During the Day:							
I repeated my affirmation(s) and consciously reprogrammed my chatter brain's self-talk.							
I reflected on the Mindful Brain Fuel daily inspiration and quote of the day.							
I initiated my action step(s) for today.							
I exercised.							
In the Evening:							
I checked off the items I completed on the daily plan.							
I answered the self-reflection question.							
I jotted down my thoughts about my journey.							
I ended my day by smiling and saying, "I am grateful for this day and the positive shift I created in my life today!"							
Bonus Activities:							
I meditated.							
I completed a random act of kindness.							
I paid it forward.							
I read an inspirational book.							
I experienced AWE!							
Other: _____							

WEEK FOUR

Mindfulness

DAY 1

Conscious Presence

This week, we're diving deeper into mindfulness, a concept we touched on back in week two. Mindfulness is simply about paying attention to the present moment without judgment. Although it seems like a trendy new buzzword, mindfulness has been around for ages, with roots in ancient practices like Hinduism, Buddhism, and even religions like Judaism and Christianity. Mindful people throughout history have been known for their calm presence, clarity of mind, and strong connection to others and the world around them.

By practicing mindfulness, you'll start noticing more about how you think, feel, and react to different situations, conversations, and even your surroundings. You'll become more open-minded, curious, and less likely to jump to conclusions. But most importantly, you'll learn to fully appreciate the present moment. After all, the present is all we've really got. The past is behind us, and the future is uncertain, so why not make the most of the here and now?

Like everything else we've talked about, mindfulness is a lifelong practice. It's not something you master overnight, but something that keeps growing as you incorporate it into your daily routine. As you continue to practice, you'll become more self-aware, gaining wisdom and insight into who you are and how you're evolving as a person. In fact, living by the golden rule (treating others how you'd like to be treated) is a perfect example of living a mindful, conscious life. It's also a surefire way to build a happier and more successful life.

You might have noticed a theme in everything we're covering—a golden thread connecting all these ideas. None of these concepts stand alone. Instead, they work together to create a beautiful tapestry that helps you raise your consciousness and transform your thinking so you can live your best life. Today's focus on Conscious Presence ties back to week two, day 1 (Wake Up!) and week three, day 5 (Observe). Take some

I'm the master of my shift!

AFFIRMATION

I direct my attention to the present moment by grounding myself in the here and now with awareness and intentionality.

WEEK FOUR

DAY 1

Unveiling Your True Self

What are your thoughts and feelings today versus how you were feeling and thinking in weeks two and three? What shifts are you experiencing?

_____
_____
_____
_____
_____
_____
_____
_____
_____
_____
_____
_____
_____
_____

*Do not dwell in the past, do not dream of the future,
concentrate the mind on the present moment.*
– Buddha

WEEK FOUR

Mindfulness

DAY 2

Intention

Think of mindfulness as millions of mirrors—like a giant disco ball that surrounds the entire earth—projecting and reflecting your thoughts, feelings, emotions, actions, and intentions throughout the universe. Picture your brain as the command center and your body as the mirror ball reflecting every one of your thoughts like diamonds glistening on the ocean or dancing off the snow on a sunny day. Whatever you project is reflected back to you—*what goes around, comes around*—*what you believe, you receive*—karma.

According to the Cleveland Clinic:

- "Your brain determines every aspect of your life and without your brain, there is no self and no awareness of the world.

- Your brain is a three-pound universe that processes 70,000 thoughts each day using 100 billion neurons that connect at more than 500 trillion points through synapses that travel 300 miles/hour.

- The signals that travel through these interconnected neurons form the basis of memories, thoughts, and feelings.

- Throughout your life your experiences create patterns of activity that explain how our brains code our thoughts, memories, skills, and sense of self."

Based on the fact that we're processing about 70,000 thoughts every day, it emphasizes the importance of becoming more mindful and creating intentional thoughts that enhance our lives. Now, in no way do I believe we have the capacity to manage all 70,000 thoughts, but even if we capture and redirect a fraction of them, it enables us to move in a more positive direction. Remember, mindfulness is the capability to bring your attention back to the present moment, so take a deep breath and set your intention to practice mindfulness.

I'm the master of my shift!

AFFIRMATION

I am a mirror for the positive energy that permeates the universe, channeling and reflecting it easily and effortlessly in every aspect of my life.

WEEK FOUR

DAY 2

Unveiling Your True Self

What is your intention for your life and what thoughts do you need to think to align with that intention?

_____

_____

_____

_____

_____

_____

_____

_____

_____

_____

_____

_____

_____

_____

_____

Our intention creates our reality.
— Wayne Dyer

WEEK FOUR

Mindfulness

DAY 3

Patience

I don't know about you, but I typically want "it" yesterday. "It" can be anything—a new car, learning how to fly a helicopter, a new pair of jeans, or learning a new skill like mindfulness. We live in an instant gratification world, and depending on what our "it" is, our needs may be satisfied within a relatively short period of time or it may take months or years. That's why learning the art and skill of patience is an essential component of living a more mindful life.

The kind of patience I'm referring to isn't "all good things come to those who wait." No, no, no. This isn't about saying "I want to be a millionaire" and just sitting back waiting for it to magically happen. If your goal is to become a millionaire, you'll need to identify the steps necessary to achieve that status, create a plan, and then proactively take action to achieve that goal. In this example, patience shows up as the perseverance to move through the challenges of conquering each step, the consistency to stick with your plan, and the deep-seated belief that you are destined to be a millionaire.

Patience in relation to mindfulness also refers to practicing self-compassion as you learn the new life skills to move in your intended direction. Patience plays a crucial role in achieving your goals and leading a happier life, but as humans, we can all struggle with maintaining patience in the face of pressure and frustrations. If an interaction or situation causes you to feel anger rising within, close your eyes and take a deep breath to refocus your attention, and repeat your patience affirmation. Just like learning any new skill, becoming aware of your patience level in various situations takes time and perseverance. The real test is practicing it in the heat of the moment.

I'm the master of my shift!

AFFIRMATION

My patience brings me inner peace and clarity, allowing me to navigate challenges with grace and ease.

WEEK FOUR

DAY 3

Unveiling Your True Self

What triggers your impatience? What's your plan for summoning patience and controlling your reactions in difficult situations?

_____
_____
_____
_____
_____
_____
_____
_____
_____
_____
_____
_____
_____
_____
_____

It does not matter how slowly you go as long as you do not stop.
– Confucius

WEEK FOUR

Mindfulness

DAY 4

Attitude

Attitude is the compass of life, the captain of your ship, the master of your destiny. It's a silent partner shaping and influencing decisions that determine the twists and turns of your journey. It is a subtle but powerful force that can steer you toward success or failure, happiness or despair. Attitude is a lens through which we view ourselves, others, and our circumstances and it governs how we interpret the world and respond to challenges and opportunities.

Your attitude encompasses your beliefs, values, and perspectives. People who choose a positive attitude embody optimism, resilience, and a growth mindset, empowering them to confront obstacles with courage and determination. Positive attitudes infuse hope, enthusiasm, and the energy to persevere through the bumps in the road along life's journey.

On the other hand, negative attitudes breed pessimism and cast a shadow over aspirations, energy, and potential. The lens of negativity distorts reality, magnifies obstacles, and diminishes opportunities. It can make you feel helpless, hopeless, and resigned to living life within self-imposed limitations and boundaries.

Fortunately, we have the capability to choose our attitude. Planting seeds of optimism, resilience, happiness, gratitude, and mindfulness in the orchard of your mind will help you raise your level of consciousness and shift your perspectives to reach your highest potential. Your attitude influences your actions, which shape the trajectory of your life.

People that exude positive attitudes are like beacons of light, drawing people to them like hummingbirds to flowers. Their positivity is contagious, spreading hope, joy, and optimism wherever they go, and they serve as reminders that even the smallest act of kindness or expression of positivity can make a world of difference.

I'm the master of my shift!

AFFIRMATION

I radiate positivity and choose to live a life of love, hope, and joy.

WEEK FOUR

DAY 4

Unveiling Your True Self

How will choosing a positive attitude change your life?

___

Whether you think you can, or you think you can't—you're right.
– Henry Ford

WEEK FOUR

Mindfulness

DAY 5

Open Mind

Cultivating a mindset of curiosity and open-mindedness opens the door to new ideas, perspectives, and experiences, while fostering innovation, empathy, and resilience. When we approach life with an open mind and heart, we are saying, "yes" to the infinite possibilities and abundance the universe has to offer. When we see life as a continual learning experience, we enrich our own viewpoints and embrace the incredible diversity that makes the world so fascinating. I associate cultivating an open mind with preparing the vast expanse of fertile soil in the orchard of your mind.

Having an open mind means you're willing to listen to new ideas and information, view the world objectively, and admit when you don't have all the answers. It doesn't mean that you'll agree with everyone, but it does mean that you will listen to other points of view through a respectful neutral lens of curiosity and empathy. An open mindset will allow you to take in new information or opposing viewpoints without preconceived bias so you can objectively compare and contrast new or different ideas, beliefs, and opinions with your own values and principles.

The result may be that you respectfully disagree or you may discover an idea to explore further. Either way, hearing other viewpoints is beneficial in validating or enlightening your own ideas or simply facilitating your investigation and study of other perspectives with an open mind and heart.

Open-mindedness also helps us broaden our understanding of how other people see the world. While we're all part of the same human race, our genetics and cultural environments shape our beliefs and values in unique ways. By exploring diverse ideas, we challenge ourselves to think differently, embrace new experiences, and grow both personally and professionally. Staying open helps cultivate optimism and bring a sense of excitement about meeting new people and trying new things. It inspires us to step outside our comfort zone, tackle challenges from fresh angles, and live a more adventurous, fulfilling life.

I'm the master of my shift!

AFFIRMATION

I embrace the diversity of perspectives and experiences around me and learn from each new encounter.

WEEK FOUR

DAY 5

Unveiling Your True Self

What deeply held beliefs or assumptions do you hold that might be limiting your ability to consider alternative perspectives or new ideas?

_____

_____

_____

_____

_____

_____

_____

_____

_____

_____

_____

_____

_____

_____

_____

Everyone you will ever meet knows something that you don't.
– Bill Nye

WEEK FOUR

Mindfulness

DAY 6

Self-Compassion

Spending too much time planning, problem-solving, daydreaming, or thinking negative or random thoughts can be stressful and lead to anxiety, sadness, or depression. But practicing self-compassion offers a pathway to healing, resilience, and well-being. By embracing kindness, understanding, and acceptance toward yourself, you will be able to transcend the limitations of self-criticism and perfectionism, choose to be emotionally resilient, and project your true self confidence and authenticity. Further, as you learn to treat yourself with kindness, understanding, and acceptance, you'll also nurture your capacity for greater empathy, connection, and compassion.

Here are a few techniques you can explore to cultivate self-compassionate and mindful behaviors. I love walking meditation because I'm experiencing the awe of nature and I'm usually with my dog and nothing compares to his pure love, energy, and zest for life. To reap the benefits of any of these, you must turn off all devices!

- Mindfulness meditation focuses on cultivating present moment awareness, observing thoughts, emotions, and bodily sensations without judgment.
- Breath awareness involves focusing on your breath; 5 counts inhale, hold for 5, and 5 counts exhale.
- Loving-kindness meditation focuses on cultivating feelings of love, compassion, and goodwill towards oneself and others through the repetition of phrases or visualizations.
- Transcendental meditation involves the use of a mantra; a word, sound, or phrase to facilitate deep relaxation and promote a state of transcendent awareness.
- Others to explore include body scan, visualization, Zen, chakra, and sound meditation.

Every type of meditation contributes to self-compassion and offers unique benefits and approaches to cultivating mindfulness, relaxation, and spiritual growth. You just need to experiment and find a practice that resonates within your soul and brings you joy.

I'm the master of my shift!

AFFIRMATION

I treat myself with the same gentleness and empathy that I would offer to a dear friend, nurturing self-compassion within my soul.

WEEK FOUR — **DAY 6**

Unveiling Your True Self

What self-care practices do you need to incorporate into your daily routine?

_____
_____
_____
_____
_____
_____
_____
_____
_____
_____
_____
_____
_____
_____
_____

Trust yourself. Create the kind of self that you will be happy to live with all your life. Make the most of yourself by fanning the tiny, inner sparks of possibility into flames of achievement.
– Golda Meir

WEEK FOUR

Mindfulness

DAY 7

Release

The idea of letting go, whether we call it release, surrender, or simply loosening our grip, offers a profound path to inner peace, freedom, and spiritual awakening. By letting go of attachments, trusting in the flow of life, and embracing divine guidance, we free ourselves from the chains of fear, resistance, and limiting beliefs. Surrendering to the universe's power, listening to the wisdom of our heart, and following the guidance of our soul reconnects us with our spirituality and taps into the infinite love and wisdom that's always within us. In surrender, we find the ultimate freedom, the freedom to be our authentic selves and live in harmony with the natural rhythm of life.

Have you ever met someone who seems to have life effortlessly flowing in their favor, with blessings and opportunities landing right in their lap? I have, and the one thing these people have in common is that they've mastered the art of not forcing things. They've learned to let go of trying to control every outcome, and instead, they align with the natural flow of divine grace and synchronicity in the universe. Since adding this practice of release to my own daily routine, I've felt a deep sense of peace in my body, along with a greater sense of freedom and alignment with my true self. Mentally, I'm more present and able to embrace life with ease and gratitude.

I encourage you to let go of the past, stop stressing about the future, and embrace the present with gratitude. When we release control, we find peace that goes beyond any circumstance, freeing us from the constant chatter in our heads and allowing us to reconnect with who we truly are.

According to Kute Blackson, author of *The Magic of Surrender*, surrendering means you're ready, open, and available. Surrendering allows you to make transformational shifts in your life and determine what life is seeking to express through you by listening to your inner voice—your soul. Surrendering isn't being passive, giving up, or a sign of weakness. It's the ability to let go of the illusion of control and tune into the flow of life. Surrendering is the secret to manifestation and one of the most powerful concepts you can practice on your way to achieving your life's highest purpose and destiny.

I'm the master of my shift!

AFFIRMATION

I live in the flow of divine grace to achieve my life's highest purpose.

WEEK FOUR — — — — — — — — — — **DAY 7**

Unveiling Your True Self

What does surrendering mean to you?

_____
_____
_____
_____
_____
_____
_____
_____
_____
_____
_____
_____
_____
_____
_____
_____

Surrender is the open-hearted participation in life and your soul's journey.
– Kute Blackson

Week 5

Resilience

The Shift Code Daily Routine Checklist

WEEK FIVE | *Resilience*	Day 1	Day 2	Day 3	Day 4	Day 5	Day 6	Day 7
In the Morning:							
I began my day by smiling and saying, "I am grateful for this day and the positive shift I'm creating in my life!"							
I read the daily action plan in my workbook.							
I made note of the focus of my affirmation(s) and self-talk for the day.							
I identified one or more action steps for the day.							
During the Day:							
I repeated my affirmation(s) and consciously reprogrammed my chatter brain's self-talk.							
I reflected on the Mindful Brain Fuel daily inspiration and quote of the day.							
I initiated my action step(s) for today.							
I exercised.							
In the Evening:							
I checked off the items I completed on the daily plan.							
I answered the self-reflection question.							
I jotted down my thoughts about my journey.							
I ended my day by smiling and saying, "I am grateful for this day and the positive shift I created in my life today!"							
Bonus Activities:							
I meditated.							
I completed a random act of kindness.							
I paid it forward.							
I read an inspirational book.							
I experienced AWE!							
Other: _____							

WEEK FIVE

Resilience

DAY 1

Elasticity

This week, we're going to dive into resilience, what it is and how to build it. I'll define resilience as the ability to bounce back from challenges and handle stress like a pro. Life is constantly giving us opportunities to stretch and grow, helping us build our mind's elasticity so we can navigate life's ups and downs with more ease. When you develop a resilient mindset, dealing with stress and tough situations becomes easier, and before you know it, you're the master of your shift!

Think of resilience like having a super-stretchy rubber band in your brain. The more flexible and elastic your mind becomes, the better you'll handle the fast pace of life, technological overload, and even the endless barrage of social media. Your mental rubber band—your mind's elasticity—helps you adapt, change your thinking, and tackle whatever comes your way. The bottom line: the more flexible your thinking, the more creative and adaptable you'll be in challenging situations. And your mind's enhanced elasticity becomes your superpower, giving you the ability to reframe old thoughts and make positive changes in your life.

You probably have lots of reasons for embarking on this 15-week journey, and maybe resilience wasn't at the top of your list, but let's not underestimate its importance. The fact that you're here, ready to make a shift, shows that you are already resilient. Despite any fears or doubts, you've chosen to participate in this program to create a brighter future and to let go of whatever's happened in the past. That takes courage and inner strength so go ahead and celebrate that! Smile and say, "Wow, I am resilient!"

Although none of us can control life's curve balls, we can nourish ourselves with healthy thoughts that increase our capability to bounce back from the tough times. If you reach a point where you need help reinforcing your resilience, don't forget you're not alone—your support team is there when you need them.

I'm the master of my shift!

AFFIRMATION

I am resilient!

WEEK FIVE

DAY 1

Unveiling Your True Self

How does resilience show up in your life?

_____
_____
_____
_____
_____
_____
_____
_____
_____
_____
_____
_____
_____
_____
_____
_____

Life doesn't get easier or more forgiving, we get stronger and more resilient.
– Steve Maraboli

WEEK FIVE

Resilience

DAY 2

Lifestyle

Lifestyle can be described as the way a person lives. This includes our approach to our health, behaviors, social patterns, and dress—each reflecting our core values, attitudes, and how we want to be perceived by others. We make lifestyle choices every day that influence our physical, mental, spiritual, and emotional well-being. Since we all have free will, we can choose wisely or foolishly, and the universe will respond in kind. Our choices test our resiliency and have a direct impact on the quality of our lives for better or worse.

If you choose a healthy lifestyle, it will enhance your resilience and help you be in top form. When you feel good—or better yet great—you think more clearly, adjust to fluid situations more easily, and generally live a more grateful, grace-filled, awe-inspiring life. We all know the drill: eat healthy foods, exercise, and get enough sleep. Some folks are better at this than others and only you know where you fall on that spectrum. My suggestion is simple: eat healthy foods, exercise, and get enough sleep. Ha! No big surprise there. You can have a cheat day now and then, but that triad is the gold standard.

Managing stress is another key piece of the puzzle when it comes to living a healthy lifestyle and building resilience. Chronic stress can wreak havoc on both your physical and mental health, so learning how to handle it effectively is crucial. Throughout this program, I'll be sharing plenty of stress-reducing activities you can try, like meditation, yoga, and more, but one thing I really want to highlight is the importance of finding a healthy balance between work and personal life. Striking that balance is a game-changer for your overall well-being.

The World Health Organization defines health as "a complete state of mental, physical and social well-being—not merely the absence of disease." Again, as human beings with free will, we can choose to adopt a healthy lifestyle or not. Our choices will determine if we reap the benefits or consequences of our decision. What do you choose?

I'm the master of my shift!

AFFIRMATION

I nourish my body, mind, and soul with healthy lifestyle choices.

WEEK FIVE

DAY 2

Unveiling Your True Self

What lifestyle changes do you need to make to enhance your resiliency?

_____

_____

_____

_____

_____

_____

_____

_____

_____

_____

_____

_____

_____

_____

_____

_____

Take care of your body. It's the only place you have to live.
– Jim Rohn

WEEK FIVE

Resilience

DAY 3

Relationship Ecosystem

Your relationship ecosystem is fragile. The relationships you nurture shape your experiences and influence your journey through life. If your relationship ecosystem is filled with trustworthy people that share your values, you and your trusted cohorts will be resilient and thrive. You will experience authentic communication, active listening, mutual support, respect for boundaries, and a commitment to continuous growth that will enrich your lives. Your shared values and sense of purpose will forge deep bonds of belonging and camaraderie as you collectively strive toward similar goals, and you'll support your allies as they support you.

The heart of your relationship ecosystem is shared values and the cornerstone of each individual relationship is trust. While shared values lay the foundation for the guiding principles that have aligned you with your cohorts, trust is the currency you exchange in each relationship. Trust creates the safe space for facilitating conversations, sharing personal stories, and being free to express your thoughts, ideas, and feelings knowing they will be held in confidence.

Trust allows you to lean on each other for support, knowing your vulnerabilities will be met with empathy and understanding. Trust cultivates accountability, encouraging each member of the ecosystem to uphold their commitments and act with integrity.

Cultivating and nurturing a robust personal relationship ecosystem requires intentionality, effort, and ongoing investment. Examples of fostering and maintaining meaningful connections with like-minded individuals include, but are not limited to,

- prioritizing open, honest communication and active listening;
- demonstrating authenticity, empathy, and respect;
- reciprocating kindness and generosity;
- respecting boundaries;
- embracing opportunities for personal development; and
- encouraging curiosity, adaptability, and exploration of new interests.

I'm the master of my shift!

AFFIRMATION

I cultivate my relationships with care and intention.

WEEK FIVE

DAY 3

Unveiling Your True Self

Revisit your support team. Do you need to add or delete any team members? Send each team member a note thanking them for their supportive relationship.

The quality of your life is the quality of your relationships.
— Tony Robbins

WEEK FIVE

Resilience

DAY 4

Time Management

Time management is an integral component of resilience because it enables us to prioritize effectively, adapt to change, reduce stress, allocate resources wisely, and achieve meaningful goals. Cultivating strong time management skills helps build the resilience needed to navigate life's challenges with grace, optimism, and perseverance.

The following ideas and tips will help you get organized to more effectively manage your time, identify your priorities, and allocate your time and resources accordingly.

- Begin each day by reading through your daily routine. This will start your day with intention, set a positive tone, and help you identify and organize your priorities.
- Open your calendar and prioritize tasks for the day/week based on urgency and importance.
- Track important dates and meetings on a physical or digital calendar.
- Break down larger tasks into smaller, more manageable steps and batch similar tasks together to increase efficiency.
- Set specific and achievable goals for each day.
- Use time blocking to schedule dedicated time for different activities.
- Eliminate distractions by silencing your phone and finding a peaceful place to work.
- Get into the habit of declining tasks or commitments that don't align with your priorities.
- Delegate tasks when possible to free up time for more important responsibilities.
- Utilize technology tools such as time tracking apps or project management software to stay organized.
- Practice mindfulness and stay present in the moment to avoid multitasking.
- Regularly evaluate and adjust your time management strategies based on what works best for you.
- Take care of your physical and mental well-being to maintain energy and focus throughout the day.

I'm the master of my shift!

AFFIRMATION

I value each moment and manage my time wisely.

WEEK FIVE

DAY 4

Unveiling Your True Self

What is your daily time management plan?

___

Time management is about life management.
– Idowu Koyenikan

WEEK FIVE

Resilience

DAY 5

Illumination

Illumination—awaken, explore, find meaning, self-discovery. Illumination lights your path toward finding clarity and insight into your purpose in life. It enables and amplifies your elasticity and, therefore, your resilience. When you shine light on your purpose, you will illuminate opportunities and possibilities that may otherwise have gone unnoticed, you can see beyond immediate obstacles, and you can envision a bright future.

At some point in life, many of us wonder why we're here. What is our life's purpose? This deeply personal and subjective question has puzzled humanity for centuries. While the answer to this question may vary greatly depending on individual beliefs, cultural backgrounds, and personal experiences, I'm sharing it with you to enhance your personal growth during this journey of self-discovery, reflection, and exploration into a deeper understanding of yourself.

If you enjoy delving deep into philosophical, religious, spiritual, humanitarian, or altruistic perspectives, then I encourage you to explore those viewpoints further. However, I'm bringing this question into the present by suggesting that you already identified many purposes for your life through the roles you named in week one. Your life has great meaning and purpose to everyone you interact with through those roles. You are leading a meaningful life through those roles and you're making a positive impact through your acts of kindness, generosity, and service to others within those roles.

I'll leave it to you to ponder the universal meaning of life but want to emphasize that you don't need the answer to that question to live with purpose and have meaning in your life now. You have purpose through your commitment to pursue your personal passions and aspirations, and to cultivate your talents and potential to the fullest. Your pursuit of illumination is building your resilience and gives your life meaning and purpose here and now.

I'm the master of my shift!

AFFIRMATION

My life is overflowing with purpose and meaning.

WEEK FIVE

DAY 5

Unveiling Your True Self

What roles did you identify in Week One? Do you need to make any changes?

_____
_____
_____
_____
_____
_____
_____
_____
_____
_____
_____
_____
_____
_____
_____
_____

The meaning of life is to discover your gift. The purpose of life is to give it away.
– William Shakespeare

WEEK FIVE

Resilience

DAY 6

Balancing the Pendulum

Is your work-life or school-life pendulum swinging wildly, swaying gracefully, or hanging peacefully in balance? If you answered swinging wildly, your life is out of balance. The elasticity of your resilience is being tested to the max, and the first thing you need to do is revisit your time management policies. After you adjust your time management schedule, explore your social relationships, recreational activities, and relaxation techniques to help reduce stress and bring balance, peace, and joy to your world.

SOCIAL

Social relationships play a pivotal role in fostering resilience. Our connections with family, friends, colleagues, and communities serve as a source of emotional, practical, and psychological support, bolstering our elasticity and ability to bounce back from challenges. In addition, our interactions in social settings gives us valuable insights, laughter, shared experiences, and meaningful conversations that foster our sense of belonging and community. Being surrounded by a supportive network of family, friends, mentors, and peers enriches us beyond measure.

RECREATION

Okay, I'm back to suggesting you exercise. Again, this can be anything to get you moving—preferably outdoors in nature—without your phone. Find something you love and "Just Do It." The benefits of combining your positive self-talk with exercise are exponential.

RELAXATION

To promote relaxation and alleviate stress, you can explore various relaxation techniques such as meditation, guided imagery, aromatherapy, deep breathing, music, art, journaling, massage, tai chi, or yoga. Find an activity that resonates with you and incorporate it into your daily routine. Remember that relaxation techniques are skills and as with any skill, your ability to relax improves with practice. Be patient with yourself and don't let your effort to relax become yet another stressor.

I'm the master of my shift!

AFFIRMATION

I am grateful for my social, recreational, and relaxation activities.

WEEK FIVE — DAY 6

Unveiling Your True Self

What activities do you engage in that give you the most pleasure and alleviate stress?

_____
_____
_____
_____
_____
_____
_____
_____
_____
_____
_____
_____
_____
_____
_____
_____

Balance is not something you find, it's something you create.
– Jana Kingsford

WEEK FIVE

Resilience

DAY 7

Self-Talk

Healthy thinking is another key component of being resilient. Maintaining nourishing thought patterns requires practicing positive self-talk. Positive self-talk cultivates a positive attitude, and that attitude helps you keep things in perspective. Change in life is inevitable, and our attitude and resilience in the face of change keeps us in balance, reduces stress, and maintains our overall well-being.

My practice of focusing my self-talk on beneficial thoughts is my key to living a happy, healthy, and abundant life. Are there times of sadness? Of course. I've lost loved ones and it hurts—deeply in my soul. I miss them every day. I grieve their loss but through my positive self-talk now hold them in my heart forever and cherish the time we had together. It's the positive attitude that I've cultivated that helps me move forward—that's resilience.

A key component of this journey is to help you develop positive self-talk and learn affirming and supportive language that encourages and uplifts you. Positive self-talk is a powerful tool that will build and reinforce your self-esteem, self-confidence, optimism, resilience, and overall happiness. By replacing negative thoughts and self-doubt with positive and empowering statements, your inner dialogue becomes a supportive and nurturing force leading you to higher and higher achievements and an innate feeling of peace, grace, and ease from deep within your soul.

I'm the master of my shift!

AFFIRMATION

I exude positivity and optimism.

WEEK FIVE — — — — — — — — — — — **DAY 7**

Unveiling Your True Self

What are the results of your positive self-talk?

Your body hears everything your mind says. Stay positive.
– Anonymous

WEEK 6

KINDNESS

The Shift Code Daily Routine Checklist

WEEK SIX | *Kindness*	Day 1	Day 2	Day 3	Day 4	Day 5	Day 6	Day 7
In the Morning:							
I began my day by smiling and saying, "I am grateful for this day and the positive shift I'm creating in my life!"							
I read the daily action plan in my workbook.							
I made note of the focus of my affirmation(s) and self-talk for the day.							
I identified one or more action steps for the day.							
During the Day:							
I repeated my affirmation(s) and consciously reprogrammed my chatter brain's self-talk.							
I reflected on the Mindful Brain Fuel daily inspiration and quote of the day.							
I initiated my action step(s) for today.							
I exercised.							
In the Evening:							
I checked off the items I completed on the daily plan.							
I answered the self-reflection question.							
I jotted down my thoughts about my journey.							
I ended my day by smiling and saying, "I am grateful for this day and the positive shift I created in my life today!"							
Bonus Activities:							
I meditated.							
I completed a random act of kindness.							
I paid it forward.							
I read an inspirational book.							
I experienced AWE!							
Other: _____							

WEEK SIX

Kindness

DAY 1

Kindness 101

Being kind isn't just about making others feel good, it makes you feel great Genuinely kind people are seen as warm, gentle, and benevolent. They tend to exhibit a variety of characteristics including, but not limited to, altruism, generosity, patience, respect, fairness, friendliness, openness, and compassion. When kindness is authentic and honest, it comes from the heart without the need for reciprocity or to look good in the eyes of others. Kindness is a valuable trait to cultivate personally and professionally, and it's imperative that it be real, sincere, and unpretentious.

Becoming and staying kind is a lifelong pursuit. Studies have shown that as some people age or gain wealth, they become less thoughtful and ignore the quality of their interactions with others. This highlights how important it is to stay grounded and remind ourselves that every person deserves respect. As Michelle Obama wisely said, "When they go low, we go high." That's a great reminder to practice thoughtfulness in the way we speak, the tone of our voice, the words we choose, and our body language. Want a life filled with grace and happiness? Just treat all living beings the way you would like to be treated.

Here are a few ways you can practice kindness:

- Show patience, empathy, understanding, gratitude, and forgiveness.
- Have meaningful conversations where you really listen.
- Make eye contact, nod your head in agreement or understanding.
- Share a friendly smile, sincere greeting, or hug (if it's appropriate).
- Speak in a warm tone of voice and use positive uplifting language.
- Be respectful and courteous, offer help when you see someone in need.
- Share your time and expertise by volunteering.
- Be generous, loving, and grateful.

Lead by example! Your acts of kindness may inspire others to be kinder and more compassionate. Who knows? You might start a chain reaction of positivity that spreads farther than you ever imagined.

I'm the master of my shift!

AFFIRMATION

I am thoughtful, kind, and respectful.

WEEK SIX   **DAY 1**

Unveiling Your True Self

How do you show kindness in your daily interactions?

_____
_____
_____
_____
_____
_____
_____
_____
_____
_____
_____
_____
_____
_____
_____
_____

Make kindness the norm.
–The Random Acts of Kindness Foundation

WEEK SIX

Kindness

DAY 2

What if I . . . ?

What if I . . . ? Interesting little question, right? What was the first thought that entered your mind when you read it? Did you go to your past, present, or future? We can't change the past, but we can learn from it. Since we don't know what the future holds, the only moment in our immediate control is the present.

You have the ability to choose how you think and behave in every moment of every day. Choose positivity and kindness and you'll live with grace and ease. Choose negativity, and your experiences will reflect that back to you. Just because you may have been treated poorly or unfairly in the past doesn't mean that you have to remain in that negative mindset or pass along those behaviors.

Today, think about what your future will be like if you choose to share kindness. Ask yourself what your future will look like if you are:

- kind and loving
- courteous and respectful
- generous and grateful
- empathetic and compassionate
- patient and peaceful
- positive and supportive
- helpful and friendly.

You can choose to live life with positivity and kindness no matter what challenges may pop up. As you embody the feelings that kindness, love, generosity, gratitude, compassion, patience, and respect stir deep within your soul, I hope a sense of peace washes over you, filling your mind and heart with love and happiness that illuminates your life with endless possibilities.

I'm the master of my shift!

AFFIRMATION

I am courteous, helpful, and friendly.

WEEK SIX

DAY 2

Unveiling Your True Self

What if I _____?

___

Don't ask "What if?" about your past. Ask "What if?" about your future.
– Brooke

WEEK SIX

Kindness

DAY 3

Empathy

Empathy, compassion, and altruism are three high-value character traits among the many qualities within the heart of kindness, and although they are related, they have distinct differences. I think the easiest way to distinguish between them is to think of them as a sliding scale where empathy can lead to compassion, which can lead to altruism. It's important to note that although feeling empathy may lead to compassion or altruism, we can feel and act on each of these independently.

EMPATHY

Empathetic people tend to be aware of other people's emotional experiences. They can look at things from different perspectives, sense the emotions of others, and imagine what it feels like to be in another person's situation. Practically speaking, it's like mentally envisioning what it might feel like to walk in someone else's shoes. Being empathetic can facilitate better communication, improve your leadership skills, and strengthen your personal and professional relationships.

COMPASSION

Compassion is when you relate to someone's plight and you act on your desire to help. For example, your friend has the flu, so you take them some soup, or you see someone in need and you lend a hand. Studies have shown that compassionate acts like giving to charity can actually activate pleasure sensors in your brain.

ALTRUISM

I think of altruism as being unselfish and doing something to help another person with no expectation of reward or personal benefit. It shows up as helping someone despite personal costs, risks, or sharing your resources even in the face of scarcity. Altruism ranges from a small act like giving your seat on the bus to someone else to a life-changing act like donating a kidney.

Research suggests that people who are more generous and caring also tend to be happier, healthier, more successful, and enjoy better relationships. So, although we all differ in our innate ability to demonstrate empathy, compassion, or altruism, it is to our benefit to increase our aptitude for expressing these values.

I'm the master of my shift!

AFFIRMATION

My heart is open and my actions are rooted in love and empathy.

WEEK SIX — — — — — — — — — — — **DAY 3**

Unveiling Your True Self

How do you feel when you're empathetic, compassionate, or altruistic? Do your feelings differ with each value?

_____
_____
_____
_____
_____
_____
_____
_____
_____
_____
_____
_____
_____
_____
_____

The great gift of human beings is that we have the power of empathy.
– Meryl Streep

WEEK SIX

Kindness

DAY 4

Testing . . . Testing

Our kindness quotient is tested in different ways every day. I'm sharing an example of a time when my kindness quotient was tested. Think about how you would have handled the situation and the degree of empathy and compassion it stirs within your soul.

The location was an old town main street with angled car parking next to the sidewalk and many mom-and-pop storefronts along the busy street. My friend and I were just getting out of the car when a man in his mid to late twenties came zooming up on his electric unicycle.

He came to an abrupt stop in front of us and asked gleefully, "Did you see me jump over that guy's leg?" My jaw dropped and I exclaimed, "What?" He pointed down the street to a man lying lifelessly across the sidewalk. He said, "It's okay, he's just a homeless guy." He zoomed off before I could respond and we watched him jump over him again.

I walked over to the man and called 911. Long story short, as I was asking the man if he was okay, his eyes fluttered open and I told him I was calling for help. He saw the phone in my hand and said, "No." Then he struggled to get up and limp down the street.

Although he was having great difficulty walking, it was obvious he didn't want to deal with the authorities. The 911 operator said they couldn't chase him down, but if he stopped to call them back.

This encounter unnerved me for many reasons: the unicyclist's brazen uncaring attitude and behavior, other people walking by this man like he didn't exist, our lack of appropriate resources for those that are homeless and possibly mentally ill, and my inability to help in this particular situation.

Our kindness, empathy, patience, and courtesy are tested in many ways every day—some small, such as sitting in traffic or long lines at the grocery or coffee shop, and some more significant, such as arguments with friends or family members. It's in these moments that we have the opportunity to act in accordance with our core values and personal mission statement or not. Sometimes we'll be successful in our quest to be a caring human being and other times we'll look back and wish we had done better. In the latter, hopefully we learn from the experience, reflect on different ways we could have responded, and be better next time.

I'm the master of my shift!

AFFIRMATION

Every act of kindness I perform makes the world a better place.

WEEK SIX — DAY 4

Unveiling Your True Self

How has your kindness been tested?
Would you handle the situation differently today than when it happened?

---

*The purpose of human life is to serve, and to show compassion
and the will to help others.*
– Albert Schweitzer

WEEK SIX

Kindness

DAY 5

Authenticity

In my opinion, it all starts with love. If you are an authentically loving person, you will be blessed with loving relationships personally and professionally. Personally, love may be finding your soulmate or having great friends that always have your back. Professionally, love shows up in the workplace as a culture where people are valued and respected.

Authentic people make genuine connections with people without expecting anything in return. They are comfortable with themselves, and their interactions are open, honest, and sincere. Their words and actions come from their heart, not their head, and they acknowledge, understand, and promote the value of building and maintaining rapport and personal connections.

Authenticity is not manipulative. It's being

- fully present when interacting with others and actively listening during conversations without thinking of how you're going to respond;

- thoughtful and non-judgmental;

- honest and acting with integrity;

- open and transparent;

- respectful and valuing diversity;

- generous with your time and resources; and

- kind.

Becoming authentic and sustaining it throughout your life takes a commitment to respect and take care of yourself first. If you don't love yourself, you won't be able to love anyone else. If you're not happy, optimistic, kind, confident, mindful, patient, or grateful you won't be able to share those attributes with anyone else. Being aware of the character traits or values you need to cultivate is necessary to enable you to have a solid foundation from which to grow. The values you want to share with the world need to be a part of you first.

I'm the master of my shift!

AFFIRMATION

My authenticity attracts genuine connections and opportunities.

WEEK SIX

DAY 5

Unveiling Your True Self

What are the behaviors you demonstrate when you're being authentic?

___

Authenticity is the alignment of head, mouth, heart, and feet—thinking, saying, feeling, and doing the same thing—consistently.
This builds trust, and followers love leaders they can trust.
– Lance Secretan

WEEK SIX

Kindness

DAY 6

Circulation

Think of never-ending circles emanating from you and returning to you—similar to the mirrors metaphor I introduced in the brain fuel segment on Week Four, Day 2, Intention. Circulation is related to intention but is different in that intention starts with your brain setting your thoughts in motion, while circulation comes from the center of your being—your heart, your soul—and is realized through your feelings and acts. And yes, just in case you're wondering, both of these concepts are related to karma—what goes around, comes around—what you believe, you receive.

There is a universal law of circulation that says if you want more, you need to give more. Since everything begins with our thoughts, we start there, but circulation needs to go deeper and become part of your belief system, your feelings, and your actions. It's been said that what you believe, you receive. I think that's true, but to me, it goes much deeper than simply believing. It's a true demonstration of living the belief. For instance,

I believe I'm a happy, optimistic, caring person and I demonstrate those characteristics in my interactions with others every day, which translates to knowing that I'm a happy, optimistic, caring person. It goes from "I believe" to "I am" as you embody and substantiate your beliefs through your actions. Just remember this sequence: think, believe, act, and then you'll receive.

Bottom line, if you want

- kindness, be kind;
- happiness, be joyful;
- peace, be peaceful;
- abundance, be grateful and generous;
- forgiveness, be forgiving.

You need to be in the energetic flow of giving and receiving. When you give, it must be from the heart with no expectations of accolades, return, or reward. The universe knows if giving is authentic or not.

I'm the master of my shift!

AFFIRMATION

I am a beacon of light and love throughout the universe.

WEEK SIX — DAY 6

Unveiling Your True Self

What do you circulate every day?

*Whatever you think the world is withholding from you,
you are withholding from the world.*
– Eckhart Tolle

WEEK SIX

Kindness

DAY 7

Random Acts of Kindness

Engaging in spontaneous acts of kindness can have numerous positive effects on both the person performing the act and the individual receiving it. For the giver, demonstrating acts of kindness can bring a sense of satisfaction and joy, stimulating the release of endorphins, often referred to as the "helper's high." This can connect us to our sense of purpose and make us feel happy.

For the receiver, random acts of kindness, no matter how small, can have a profound impact on their day and even inspire them to pass it on to others. Random acts of kindness not only uplift individuals but also contributes to building a more caring and connected society.

My challenge to you is to perform five random acts of kindness each week (anonymously when possible). Ideas:

- Leave a huge tip for a small check.
- Pay for the person in line behind you.
- Volunteer at your local animal shelter or food bank.
- Do something for someone else that requires time and effort on your part.
- Compliment a stranger.
- Donate clothes you no longer need.
- Offer to help a neighbor with their groceries.
- Send a handwritten letter or thank-you card to a friend.
- Bring treats to your coworkers.
- Buy a meal for a homeless person.
- Leave a positive review for a small business.
- Pick up litter in your neighborhood.
- Call a family member just to say you love them.
- Donate to a cause you care about.

I'm the master of my shift!

AFFIRMATION

My random acts of kindness create ripples of joy and positivity in the world, touching hearts and inspiring others to do the same.

WEEK SIX — DAY 7

Unveiling Your True Self

What random acts of kindness do you regularly practice?

_____
_____
_____
_____
_____
_____
_____
_____
_____
_____
_____
_____
_____
_____

Imagine a world where you can succeed by being nice. Where we all pay it forward. Where people look out for each other. It all starts with an act.
– Random Acts of Kindness Foundation

WEEK 7

GRATITUDE

The Shift Code Daily Routine Checklist

WEEK SEVEN	*Gratitude*	Day 1	Day 2	Day 3	Day 4	Day 5	Day 6	Day 7
In the Morning:								
	I began my day by smiling and saying, "I am grateful for this day and the positive shift I'm creating in my life!"							
	I read the daily action plan in my workbook.							
	I made note of the focus of my affirmation(s) and self-talk for the day.							
	I identified one or more action steps for the day.							
During the Day:								
	I repeated my affirmation(s) and consciously reprogrammed my chatter brain's self-talk.							
	I reflected on the Mindful Brain Fuel daily inspiration and quote of the day.							
	I initiated my action step(s) for today.							
	I exercised.							
In the Evening:								
	I checked off the items I completed on the daily plan.							
	I answered the self-reflection question.							
	I jotted down my thoughts about my journey.							
	I ended my day by smiling and saying, "I am grateful for this day and the positive shift I created in my life today!"							
Bonus Activities:								
	I meditated.							
	I completed a random act of kindness.							
	I paid it forward.							
	I read an inspirational book.							
	I experienced AWE!							
	Other: _____							

WEEK SEVEN

Gratitude

DAY 1

Mindset

Now that you're several weeks into this practice you may be wondering when you're going to see massive improvements in your life. You're being diligent about practicing the daily routine, repeating your affirmations, and giving thought to the question of the day but may not yet be feeling or seeing your intended shifts. Well, my friend, change generally comes in tiny increments over your lifetime, but don't despair, you're gradually creating new neural pathways that will result in a more positive mindset. This is a lifetime practice so don't give up!

Thank goodness I've cultivated a positive mindset that helps me get through challenging situations because as I began writing Week Five's theme of resilience, life presented me with the opportunity to practice resilience and all the topics I'm sharing with you in this book. My house became uninhabitable due to a water leak because it took the HOA over two and a half weeks to respond to my requests to send someone to find the leak. When they finally came out it took the plumber less than thirty minutes to find the leak, but by that time the water had spread under the laminate flooring and through the original tiles to the concrete slab. It seemed at every turn there was a new challenge, first mold and then being told that all the original flooring throughout the house had asbestos and needed to be removed. I had to put all my furniture and belongings in storage and my dog and I moved to a hotel.

Aside from the death of loved ones, this incident was the most traumatic experience of my life because every new discovery kept spiraling into more damage, more expense, more stress, and it threatened one of our most basic needs—a safe place to live. The stress even caused my dog to get pancreatitis and me to go to the ER with chest pains. Fortunately, we are both fine. Throughout this experience, there were definitely moments when I was overwhelmed. I acknowledged and respected my rollercoaster of emotions, kept practicing my daily routine, and with emotional support from a dear friend I persevered.

Stressful situations like this challenge our ability to be grateful but it's very important to find things to be thankful for no matter how small they may be. For instance, I focused my gratitude practice on how blessed I am to have such a special friend in my life, for having homeowner's insurance, finding competent people to repair my home, living in Southern California and being able to walk at the beach, my awesome dog Bentley, my health, and the inspiration and determination to continue writing this book to share my gratitude practice with you.

I'm the master of my shift!

AFFIRMATION

My attitude is gratitude!

WEEK SEVEN — DAY 1

Unveiling Your True Self

How would you describe your gratitude mindset?

_____
_____
_____
_____
_____
_____
_____
_____
_____
_____
_____
_____
_____
_____
_____

**Gratitude makes sense of your past, brings peace for today,
and creates a vision for tomorrow.
- Melody Beattie**

WEEK SEVEN

Gratitude

DAY 2

Mother Nature

Gratitude is more than giving thanks for our blessings and abundance. Gratitude is a fundamental mindset for maintaining balance in difficult situations. My attitude of gratitude contributes to my physical and mental health, resilience, and ability to live with peace, grace, and ease. I consider gratitude an essential core value and a foundational element for life.

As you are contemplating the role of gratitude within your life, I suggest you commune with Mother Nature. Being outdoors in nature is good for our souls. It gives us an opportunity to connect with our inner selves and provides a space for solitude, reflection, and renewal. Nature is inspiring and can get our creative juices flowing, allowing us to explore new ideas and perspectives. It's amazing what getting away from the hustle, bustle, technology, and noise of daily life can do. My gratitude vibes are always more intense when I walk on the beach, through a beautiful mountain meadow, or around my neighborhood park.

Go to your favorite place—that place in nature that regenerates your soul. Take time to soak in the ambiance—the sights, sounds, smells, and feelings of peace and joy this place gives you. Close your eyes and create the movie of your life including your past, present, and future. Focus on everything you have to be grateful for, i.e., nature, family, friends, relationships, mentors, pets, accomplishments, achievements, life lessons, opportunities, experiences, challenges, setbacks and adversities you have overcome, adventures, career, and the basic comforts of food, clothing, and shelter.

As you reflect on your past, this exercise may bring up some experiences you may want to forget. However, if you can find one tiny speck of gratitude and give thanks for any lessons learned, you can release the negativity surrounding the experience and choose to move forward with a gratitude mindset. Envision your future with the knowledge you gained from each life lesson and be thankful for your newfound wisdom. Cultivating gratitude for accomplishments and success is easy, but being able to find gratitude in your challenges will be your greatest achievement toward becoming more enlightened, resilient, and empowered.

I'm the master of my shift!

AFFIRMATION

I appreciate my journey and am grateful for every experience.

WEEK SEVEN — DAY 2

Unveiling Your True Self

What are you grateful for?

_____
_____
_____
_____
_____
_____
_____
_____
_____
_____
_____
_____
_____
_____
_____
_____

Gratitude is not only the greatest of virtues but the parent of all others.
- Cicero

WEEK SEVEN

Gratitude

DAY 3

Relationships

We all have many relationships in our lives, ranging from smiling at a stranger as you walk down a busy street to deeply loving someone such as your life partner, parent, sibling, or close friend. Expressing gratitude for your relationships is powerful and can change your life. Showing gratitude improves your health, increases your capacity for being less judgmental and more empathetic, and helps build your positive thinking neural pathways. When gratitude becomes your default position, your positive thoughts override negativity leading to permanent changes in your brain.

IDENTIFY AND PRIORITIZE RELATIONSHIPS

1) **Toxic Relationships**
   I hesitated to add this section, but if we're being honest there may be someone that isn't healthy for you to have in your life. If that's the case it's time to let them go so you can continue on your path to a bright future filled with love and success.

2) **Passing Relationships**
   Next, give thanks for the acquaintances and friends that have passed through your life as a part of your career, experiences, and adventures. Although many of these relationships may have been intensely rewarding and beneficial at the time they occurred, they may not have been meant for a lifetime. Passing relationships are wonderful experiences, but they simply come and go with the flow of events and adventures throughout your life.

3) **Lifetime Relationships**
   Finally, turn your attention to the handful of incredibly special relationships that are meant for a lifetime. Nurture and give thanks for these! They are a blessing and will enrich your life in unimaginable ways. Once you have identified these very special people, reach out to them and express your gratitude. Let them know what they mean to you and how they make your life better. Sharing your feelings with them will let them know they are appreciated and strengthen your emotional bond. Expressing your feelings will also release endorphins that make you both feel good and put you in a positive and grateful state of mind.

I'm the master of my shift!

AFFIRMATION

I am blessed and thankful for the people who enrich my life.

WEEK SEVEN — DAY 3

Unveiling Your True Self

Who are you grateful for and why?

_____
_____
_____
_____
_____
_____
_____
_____
_____
_____
_____
_____
_____
_____
_____
_____

Feeling gratitude and not expressing it is like wrapping a present and not giving it.
– William Arthur Ward

WEEK SEVEN

Gratitude

DAY 4

Achievements

Today is a day of celebration for all that you've accomplished in life. Reflect on your achievements—large and small—and express gratitude to yourself and everyone that contributed to your success. Although your accomplishments may seem like an individual effort, there were others that helped you at some point along your road to success. Think back to Tiger, Michael, and Serena. Even though they each excel individually in their respective sport, they all have a team supporting them behind the scenes.

Acknowledging and expressing gratitude for your achievements is a powerful practice that will reinforce your positive mindset and strengthen your relationships. Here are a few ways to express gratitude for your achievements:

Reflect
Write about the challenges you've overcome, the lessons you learned, and the people who supported you along the way.

Celebrate
Host a party to share your success and acknowledge the contributions of your team.

Pay It Forward
Help someone else achieve their goals by becoming a mentor or volunteer.

Gifts
Consider giving personalized gifts as tokens of appreciation.

Bucket List
For your extraordinary achievements, pop the Champagne and tick an item off your bucket list, i.e., take a trip around the world, skydive, scuba dive at the Great Barrier Reef, learn a new language, take a cooking class in Italy, write a book, or start a new business. Do something that makes your heart sing, you deserve it!

I'm the master of my shift!

AFFIRMATION

Every day, I find new reasons to be thankful.

WEEK SEVEN
DAY 4

Unveiling Your True Self

Which of your achievements make you most proud and why?

_____
_____
_____
_____
_____
_____
_____
_____
_____
_____
_____
_____
_____
_____
_____

Behind every successful individual is a supportive team cheering them on.
– Anonymous

WEEK SEVEN

Gratitude

DAY 5

Needs versus Wants

Your gratitude practice needs to be grounded in being thankful for what you have, not what you want. Be thankful for the basics—food, water, air, shelter, and clothing. For instance, give thanks for being able to pay your rent or mortgage and for other necessities such as groceries, clothing, utilities, phone, car, and health insurance. Focus on the here and now—the present moment. Live in the blessings of today, not in the longing for the superficial materialistic trappings promoted on social media. It's not what you have; it's who you are that counts.

Now I'm not saying that wanting something is bad. In fact, wanting a better future and a happy life is an awesome goal and something important to strive for. Figure out what will bring you joy and enhance your life, such as finding your soulmate, a different job, or perhaps a larger circle of friends. Once you have the important things in life covered, you can splurge on material things that aren't necessary but would be fun like vacations, dining out, a McMansion, fancy car, or designer clothes.

Let's say that our basic needs—food, water, air, shelter, and clothing—score a 10 on a scale of 1—10, with 10 being absolutely essential. Now list everything you want and give each item a rating of 1—10, asking yourself if the item is essential to your survival as a human being. Since we all need relationships, you'll probably give family and friends a 10 as well. However, when you turn your attention beyond the basics to the things that would be nice to have, your scores will begin to reveal your priorities and you'll see what motivates you and what brings you joy.

As you list your wants, you may discover that some of the things you think you want may not get you where you want to go in life. For instance, let's say you're looking at $2,000 designer shoes but your scores indicate that a bigger home is a higher priority. You may decide to buy less expensive shoes and bank the extra cash toward your new home. Life gives us many opportunities for choosing between needs and wants, and fortunately, we are blessed with the decision-making capability to evaluate how our choice will affect our life.

I'm the master of my shift!

AFFIRMATION

I am grateful for everything I have and the infinite abundance in my life.

WEEK SEVEN — DAY 5

Unveiling Your True Self

What do you need? What do you want? Will what you want improve your life, make you happy, or make you a better person?

_____
_____
_____
_____
_____
_____
_____
_____
_____
_____
_____
_____
_____
_____
_____

Gratitude turns what we have into enough.
– Aesop

WEEK SEVEN

Gratitude

DAY 6

Adventures

What pops into your mind when you hear the word adventure? Do you picture something thrilling or risky, like climbing Mt. Everest, BASE jumping, or racing at LeMans? While those might be among the first things we think of, I challenge you to broaden your perspective. Adventures can be those spontaneous, fun, and sometimes unexpected moments that pop up in our everyday lives. Take vacations, for example. Every trip I've taken feels like an adventure—exploring new places, meeting new people, and trying new things. Even taking a wrong turn can turn into an adventure since it leads you somewhere unknown.

With this wider view in mind, think back on the adventures in your life, starting from childhood up to now, like the time you and your friends explored a nearby forest pretending to be fearless adventurers. Or the time you finished a century (100 mile) bike ride, learned to drive, or moved to a different state or country. Maybe you've gone on far-flung journeys to exotic places, tried activities like spelunking, mountain climbing, or ziplining. Or maybe your adventures have been more low-key, like a lazy afternoon at the park, a thrilling day at an amusement park, or even navigating a crazy traffic jam.

No matter what shape or size your adventures have been, they've all brought opportunities to learn something new and find gratitude in the moment. As you reflect on them, think about the people you shared those special moments with and how you can still feel the laughter and emotions.

When you embrace this expanded idea of adventure—welcoming life's surprises and uncertainties with curiosity and a bit of humor—you open yourself up to being grateful for all the new, exciting, and even challenging experiences that come your way. You also start appreciating those little adventures that nudge you outside your comfort zone.

I'm the master of my shift!

AFFIRMATION

I am grateful for all my experiences and adventures.

WEEK SEVEN

DAY 6

Unveiling Your True Self

What adventure has been your biggest life lesson?

_____
_____
_____
_____
_____
_____
_____
_____
_____
_____
_____
_____
_____
_____

The whole of life, from the moment you are born to the moment you die, is a process of learning.
– Jiddu Krishnamurti

WEEK SEVEN

Gratitude

DAY 7

Exploration

According to Kelly Barron, mindfulness instructor for eMindful Inc. and UCLA's Mindful Awareness Research Center, there are four ways to explore gratitude:

1) **Notice Beauty**
   How do your physical senses recognize and experience beauty? Explore how you notice something lovely today. What part of that process sparks gratitude?

2) **Notice Creativity**
   Notice an innovative idea you have today, in any area of your life—a new way of doing something, a response to a question somebody asks you, your perception of another person's behavior, your understanding of something you read, a new recipe you invent. How do innovative ideas feel in your body when they arise?

3) **Notice Tenderness**
   Notice acts of tenderness between others—a couple, parent-child, person-pet—or bring to mind a favorite scene of tenderness from a movie, television show, or book. How do these moments resonate for you?

4) **Notice Connection**
   How does it feel to have a new idea that might benefit your community? Have you generated energy around your ideas and connected with others who can help move it forward?

I encourage you to explore gratitude more deeply with the multitude of books and websites dedicated to the topic. Start by watching the inspiring film *Gratitude Revealed* by Louie Schwartzberg. It's available at https://gratituderevealed.com/.

I'm the master of my shift!

AFFIRMATION

Gratitude fills my heart and uplifts my spirit.

WEEK SEVEN — DAY 7

Unveiling Your True Self

How do you define gratitude?

*Gratitude is a powerful catalyst for happiness.
It's the spark that lights a fire of joy in your soul.*
– Amy Collette

Week 8

Forgiveness

The Shift Code Daily Routine Checklist

WEEK EIGHT | *Forgiveness*	Day 1	Day 2	Day 3	Day 4	Day 5	Day 6	Day 7
In the Morning:							
I began my day by smiling and saying, "I am grateful for this day and the positive shift I'm creating in my life!"							
I read the daily action plan in my workbook.							
I made note of the focus of my affirmation(s) and self-talk for the day.							
I identified one or more action steps for the day.							
During the Day:							
I repeated my affirmation(s) and consciously reprogrammed my chatter brain's self-talk.							
I reflected on the Mindful Brain Fuel daily inspiration and quote of the day.							
I initiated my action step(s) for today.							
I exercised.							
In the Evening:							
I checked off the items I completed on the daily plan.							
I answered the self-reflection question.							
I jotted down my thoughts about my journey.							
I ended my day by smiling and saying, "I am grateful for this day and the positive shift I created in my life today!"							
Bonus Activities:							
I meditated.							
I completed a random act of kindness.							
I paid it forward.							
I read an inspirational book.							
I experienced AWE!							
Other: _____							

WEEK EIGHT

Forgiveness

DAY 1

Acknowledge

Forgiveness is one of the greatest gifts you can give yourself and to others and, choosing to let go of resentment and anger can lift your spirit and free your soul to live in peace. According to the Mayo Clinic, forgiveness doesn't mean forgetting or excusing harm done to you. Nor does it mean you need to make up with the person who caused the harm. But forgiving does bring a kind of peace that allows you to focus on yourself and help you get on with your life.

While the memory of a hurtful experience may never fully disappear, working on forgiveness can help you break free from its emotional hold. Letting go of grudges and resentment brings a wealth of benefits, from boosting your health and self-esteem to improving relationships and reducing stress and anger.

Forgiveness is all about focusing on what you can control right now. It takes commitment, determination, and a lot of practice, but it's worth the effort. Start by recognizing the value of forgiveness and how it can make a positive impact on your life. Then, think of a specific incident and the person you want to forgive (and don't forget, you might need to forgive yourself too). Acknowledge your feelings around what happened and understand how those emotions have shaped your life. Choose to forgive and release any power or control that person or situation has lingering over you.

Sometimes, the hurt can cut deep—whether a family member betrayed your trust, you were the victim of a crime, or you were bullied. Even small, inconsiderate remarks can sting and be tough to let go of. But regardless of whether the wound is big or small, forgiveness isn't always easy. Be patient with yourself. Forgiving someone can be a tough road, and it's often an ongoing process. You may need to revisit old wounds and practice forgiveness again and again, but with time, it can help heal those emotional scars.

I'm the master of my shift!

AFFIRMATION

Forgiving myself and others transforms my life and brings me peace.

WEEK EIGHT

DAY 1

Unveiling Your True Self

Who and/or what incidents need forgiveness in your life?

___

___

___

___

___

___

___

___

___

___

___

___

___

___

___

If we really want to love, we must learn to forgive.
– Mother Teresa

WEEK EIGHT

Forgiveness

DAY 2

Understand

Forgiveness is a process that takes courage and understanding. Courage to review the incident objectively, and the empathy/understanding to step into someone else's shoes and try to grasp their behavior and perspective. As you go through this process, your resilience and capability for elasticity in your thinking will be tested (Week Five, Day 1). Ultimately, your newfound ability to see things differently will boost your self-esteem, build your confidence, and open you up to the possibility of forgiving—both yourself and others.

The truth is forgiveness benefits you most of all. When you reflect on past hurts and try to understand the how and why, you might not always be able to make sense of everything or fully reconcile what happened. But by approaching the process with an open heart and a loving mindset, it becomes just a bit easier to let go and move forward. If you're in the process of forgiving yourself, try to imagine yourself wrapped in a warm, soft blanket of love, reminding yourself that you are worthy of forgiveness and deserve to be loved.

As you practice forgiveness, be mindful not to speak negatively about those who have hurt you. That kind of negative talk only stirs up more anger and doesn't help heal the pain. While you might never fully understand or forgive someone, it's important to create a mental neutral zone where that person no longer has the power to stir your emotions. When you think about the situation, stay connected to your loving, open heart and imagine placing the incident in a helium balloon. Let it float far away—*or pop it!*—whatever feels better to you.

You can incorporate forgiveness into your daily life by practicing simple acts of kindness. Don't honk in traffic, smile at strangers, or try one of the random acts of kindness mentioned in Week Six, Day 7. When you choose to spread love and positivity into the world, you naturally become less reactive, more understanding, and better equipped to forgive.

I'm the master of my shift!

AFFIRMATION

My heart is open to forgiveness and love.

WEEK EIGHT — DAY 2

Unveiling Your True Self

Pick a particular situation that needs forgiveness. As you look at it from different perspectives, what have you learned?

_____
_____
_____
_____
_____
_____
_____
_____
_____
_____
_____
_____
_____
_____
_____
_____

Forgiveness is not weak. It takes courage to face and overcome powerful emotions.
– Desmond Tutu

WEEK EIGHT

Forgiveness

DAY 3

Accept Responsibility

Accepting responsibility can sometimes be a challenge and is always a character-building moment. Today, I'm presenting three scenarios that involve looking at forgiveness from different perspectives. In all three of these instances, you need to accept responsibility and decide how to handle the situation.

1) **You need to apologize.**
   Think of a time in your life when you were unkind, said words you regret, broke something owned by someone else but no one saw you do it, accidentally dented a car in a parking lot, or something else. Would you accept responsibility, apologize, and pay for damages—especially if no one knows you did it?

A note about apologies. They should be sincere and from the heart. They may be accepted by the person to whom you're apologizing or not, but in either case, do not try and justify your actions. All the other person is interested in is your acknowledgment and remorse for your part in the event. An apology is about them, not you. If they choose to vent, just listen, and don't speak other than to say you're sorry.

2) **You need to forgive someone else.**
   Think of an instance where another person's words hurt you. Try to look at it from the other person's perspective. What was your role? What have you learned from this experience?

   Obviously, if the incident involved bodily harm, this escalates to another level and your first priority is recovering physically. Once you're able, you should consult a mental health professional to help with your recovery.

3) **You need to forgive yourself.**
   Recall an instance in your life where you feel guilt. You wish you had handled a situation differently but can't reconcile or apologize because the other person is no longer in your life. In this instance, this isn't about condoning your behavior or absolving your accountability. It's about recognizing we are imperfect and capable of learning from our mistakes. How will you learn from this mistake and open the door to personal healing?

I'm the master of my shift!

AFFIRMATION

I am responsible for my words and conduct and act with integrity.

WEEK EIGHT

DAY 3

Unveiling Your True Self

How will you accept responsibility for your actions from this point forward?

_____
_____
_____
_____
_____
_____
_____
_____
_____
_____
_____
_____
_____
_____
_____

Mistakes are always forgivable if one has the courage to admit them.
– Bruce Lee

WEEK EIGHT

Forgiveness

DAY 4

Release Resentment

Resentment is a complex mix of anger, disappointment, and bitterness and stems from perceived injustices, unmet expectations, or unresolved conflicts. Unlike losing your temper in the moment, resentment is a slow-burning emotion that can grow over time, feeding on past hurts and grievances. Resentment can strain relationships, create barriers to communication, distort our perception of others and ourselves, and make it difficult to move forward and embrace positive experiences.

Although we know it isn't healthy to hold on to resentment, it can be difficult to let go. Studies have shown that when people are presented with a hypothetical situation to imagine forgiving someone, the neural pathways in their brain responsible for empathy show increased activity. This highlights that if you can show empathy toward the person that hurt you, it can help you open up to releasing resentment and begin the process of forgiveness.

To release resentment, you must first acknowledge it and be aware of the feelings and emotions surrounding it. Once you've identified your feelings and emotions, you need to find a way to express them, i.e., talk to a member of your support team or a professional therapist, write them down, and then have a ceremony to burn them, go to a rage room, hit a punching bag at the gym, or make a beautiful piece of art. The point is to do something to release that negative energy from your mind and body.

AFFIRMATION

I'm the master of my shift!

I embrace forgiveness, let go of anger and resentment, and welcome new beginnings.

WEEK EIGHT

Unveiling Your True Self

DAY 4

What activities would you like to engage in to release resentment?

To carry a grudge is like being stung to death by one bee.
– William Walton

WEEK EIGHT

Forgiveness

DAY 5

Heal

Healing and forgiveness go hand in hand like peanut butter and jelly or maybe more like kale and green smoothies. Sure, they're good for you, but they take some time to get used to. Healing, as part of forgiveness, is not a one-time event. It's more like a marathon where you're carrying a backpack full of grudges and emotional baggage that you slowly drop off along the way and when you reach the finish line, you feel a lot lighter!

So, what does healing actually mean when it comes to forgiveness? It's about letting go of the anger, resentment, and that mental list of "how they wronged me" you've been carrying around. You know, the one you sometimes stew over in the shower or while stuck in traffic. But here's the catch—you're not doing it for them—you're doing it for you! Holding onto grudges is exhausting. It's like trying to run with a boulder strapped to your back: it's heavy, it slows you down, and frankly, it's not your best look.

Many people find that writing down their experience and then having a ceremony to shred or burn their documentation has a freeing effect and helps them move on. If you choose to try this, be sure to include the following:

- A complete description of the incident from your perspective as well as the other person's point of view.

- Include everything you would like to say to the other person.

- Write down why you're choosing to forgive them.

- Have a ceremony to shred or burn the document to release all negativity.

- As you destroy the document, you can say, "I choose to forgive and release all negativity surrounding this incident. I am free and I'm moving forward as a confident, loving, and compassionate person."

Forgiving is tough, but healing is the sweet reward at the end of it all. It's the feeling of lightness, peace, and maybe even a little joy sneaking back into your life. So go ahead, drop that baggage. You don't need it where you're going!

I'm the master of my shift!

AFFIRMATION

I am grateful for the healing power of forgiveness.

WEEK EIGHT

DAY 5

Unveiling Your True Self

What steps will you take to heal from past grievances?

_____
_____
_____
_____
_____
_____
_____
_____
_____
_____
_____
_____
_____
_____

As I walked out the door toward the gate that would lead to my freedom, I knew if I didn't leave my bitterness and hatred behind, I'd still be in prison.
– Nelson Mandela

WEEK EIGHT

Forgiveness

DAY 6

Set Boundaries

Setting boundaries is like setting up personal "no trespassing" signs for your well-being. It's a process that takes patience, practice, and a bit of self-reflection. First, take some time to think about what's important to you, your needs and values (cue Week One, Day 4 on Core Values). Think about how certain people or situations push your buttons or make you feel uncomfortable. Once you know what's okay and what's definitely not in different areas of your life, (i.e., work, relationships, or social settings), you can start setting those much-needed limits.

Here are a few examples of boundary-busting behaviors:

- Oversharing personal details with a coworker who clearly didn't ask for them.

- Pressuring someone to talk when they've made it clear they need space to process.

- Giving out hugs or pats on the back when someone has already told you they're not into it.

- Getting into someone's space without asking or standing way too close even though they're clearly uncomfortable.

- Expecting immediate replies to texts or calls, even when the other person's busy or off the clock.

- Lingering at a friend's house long after it's clear they're ready to wrap things up.

- Borrowing things without asking or not returning borrowed items (we all know that person).

- Messaging coworkers outside of agreed-upon work hours.

Once you've got your boundaries in place, it's all about letting people know when they've crossed the line (politely, of course). Use "I" statements like "I feel uncomfortable when you…" to make your point clear. And if they forget or ignore your boundaries? Stand firm, keep reminding them, and stay consistent. By calling out boundary-crossing behavior, you're looking out for your own mental health and creating more respectful relationships.

I'm the master of my shift!

AFFIRMATION

I set personal boundaries that create balance and harmony in my life.

WEEK EIGHT   DAY 6

Unveiling Your True Self

What are your personal and professional boundaries?

_____
_____
_____
_____
_____
_____
_____
_____
_____
_____
_____
_____
_____
_____

Daring to set boundaries is about having the courage to love ourselves, even when we risk disappointing others.
– Brene Brown

WEEK EIGHT

Forgiveness

DAY 7

Forgiveness Pledge

The following is from the International Forgiveness Institute (IFI), a world-wide, not-for-profit organization dedicated to helping people gain knowledge about forgiveness and to use that knowledge for personal, group, and societal renewal.

They believe that forgiveness is a choice. If you have been deeply hurt by another, you can choose to forgive rather than hold on to debilitating anger and resentment. In doing so, an amazing transformation begins. The black clouds of anxiety and depression give way to enhanced self-esteem and genuine feelings of hopefulness. When you forgive, you may benefit the person you forgive, but by liberating yourself from pain and sorrow, you can reclaim your life and find the peace that your anger had stolen.

The IFI is convinced that anyone—individuals, families, communities, even governments—can experience the extraordinary benefits of forgiveness. By learning to forgive and committing to live the forgiving life, we can all help restore healthy emotions, rebuild relationships, and establish more peaceful communities around the world. Become a "Peace Builder" now and adopt the Forgiveness Pledge.

The IFI Forgiveness Pledge:

1) Forgiveness is an important part of my life.

2) I will do my best to forgive people from my family of origin.

3) I will be a conduit of forgiveness in my family.

4) I will forgive in the workplace and do my best to create a forgiving atmosphere.

5) I will encourage forgiveness in my place of worship so that it is a forgiving community.

6) I will do my best to plant and promote forgiveness in my wider community.

7) I commit to living the forgiving life.

You can sign this pledge online at https://internationalforgiveness.com/forgiveness-pledge/

I'm the master of my shift!

AFFIRMATION

Forgiveness sets me free and brings love, peace, and joy into my heart.

WEEK EIGHT

DAY 7

Unveiling Your True Self

How will forgiveness contribute to your legacy?

_____
_____
_____
_____
_____
_____
_____
_____
_____
_____
_____
_____
_____
_____
_____
_____
_____

Listen, people can do unforgivable things, but you have to let it go and say, look, we're all human beings. We make mistakes.
– Jennifer Aniston

WEEK 9

HUMILITY

The Shift Code Daily Routine Checklist

WEEK NINE | *Humility*	Day 1	Day 2	Day 3	Day 4	Day 5	Day 6	Day 7
In the Morning:							
I began my day by smiling and saying, "I am grateful for this day and the positive shift I'm creating in my life!"							
I read the daily action plan in my workbook.							
I made note of the focus of my affirmation(s) and self-talk for the day.							
I identified one or more action steps for the day.							
During the Day:							
I repeated my affirmation(s) and consciously reprogrammed my chatter brain's self-talk.							
I reflected on the Mindful Brain Fuel daily inspiration and quote of the day.							
I initiated my action step(s) for today.							
I exercised.							
In the Evening:							
I checked off the items I completed on the daily plan.							
I answered the self-reflection question.							
I jotted down my thoughts about my journey.							
I ended my day by smiling and saying, "I am grateful for this day and the positive shift I created in my life today!"							
Bonus Activities:							
I meditated.							
I completed a random act of kindness.							
I paid it forward.							
I read an inspirational book.							
I experienced AWE!							
Other: _____							

WEEK NINE

Humility

DAY 1

Self-Awareness

Humility is defined in the *Oxford Dictionary* as a "modest or low view of one's own importance." Although I understand *Oxford's* definition on an intellectual level, I disagree with the premise that we should have a "low view" of our own importance. We should hold ourselves and every human in high regard while on our earthly journey.

Humility—the art of being humble—begins with self-awareness and being grounded in the reality that no one is perfect, no one person has all the answers, and no human is better than another. Our DNA, cultural background, strengths, weaknesses, and life experiences allow each of us to contribute to society in our own unique way. All human beings are connected through the energetic flow of the universe no matter their wealth, celebrity, career, social status, cultural background, educational level, occupation, or their gender. In addition, this energy connects us to every living thing on earth and that brings clarity to Oxford's definition of humility. In that respect, we should be in awe of the world around us and have a modest view of our own importance when compared to the infinite flow throughout the universe.

Being humble is one of the greatest virtues we can cultivate as human beings, and true strength and greatness comes from serving others without seeking glory. As the cornerstone of wisdom and leadership, humility is demonstrated through having a mindset of modesty, empathy, and respect. Ultimately, recognizing the value of working together for the greater good is one of the most precious gifts you can give yourself and the world.

THINK BIG
SHARE SUCCESS
STAY HUMBLE

I'm the master of my shift!

AFFIRMATION

I embrace humility and appreciate the strengths and contributions of others.

WEEK NINE | DAY 1

Unveiling Your True Self

What would the world look like if everyone was humble?

_____
_____
_____
_____
_____
_____
_____
_____
_____
_____
_____
_____
_____
_____
_____

Being humble is not to think less of oneself, but to think of oneself less.
– Jeff Boss

WEEK NINE

Humility

DAY 2

Open to Feedback

One trait of humbleness is being open to and receptive of feedback and constructive criticism from others. Humble people view feedback as an opportunity for growth and self-improvement, rather than as a threat to their ego. They have cultivated the ability to step out of their ego mind and turn off their chatter brain and emotions so they can listen to feedback with an open mind and heart.

Learning this skill can be difficult because we are prewired with a bias toward thinking our work is great and our actions are acceptable. So, we tend to lean in to defending ourselves. However, once you learn to stand back and put down the defense barrier, you can be neutral, calm, and unemotional when presented with the opportunity for feedback. By releasing emotions and personal bias, you'll increase your ability to listen to the feedback logically and objectively.

A few benefits of inviting feedback include increasing your self-awareness and ability to:

- listen objectively and welcome different perspectives,
- overcome personal biases
- regulate your emotions and set your personal feelings aside,
- make better decisions, and
- be mindful and empathetic.

Having a better understanding of how others receive information from you can help you become a better communicator. Feedback is a two-way street and includes giving as well as receiving. If you're the person giving feedback, all of the recommendations shared above are applicable as well. Now that you're more conscious of feedback, you'll notice that feedback is everywhere—from one-on-one conversations with family and friends to professional business meetings to social settings. When someone honks at a car that cuts them off, they are giving feedback. When you tip someone for outstanding service, you are giving them feedback. Your challenge is to use feedback as a personal motivational tool.

I'm the master of my shift!

AFFIRMATION

I am open to learning from every person and experience.

WEEK NINE

DAY 2

Unveiling Your True Self

What are the advantages of adjusting and adapting to feedback and constructive criticism?

___

*Courage is what it takes to stand up and speak;
courage is also what it takes to sit down and listen.*
—Winston Churchill

WEEK NINE

Humility

DAY 3

Appreciation

Humble people let their actions speak louder than words. They stay grounded in gratitude, appreciating the blessings and opportunities life throws their way, while also acknowledging the support of others in their success. Yep, here I go again, reminding you that gratitude is the foundation of, well, just about everything. It's important to be thankful for where we are and what we have because life can change in the blink of an eye—for better or for worse.

Take Joe, for example. Joe, a homeless man, minding his own business, when a young volunteer named Maggie asked if he needed help. His response: "Don't we all?"

That answer stopped Maggie in her tracks. She'd just started volunteering at the local shelter and wasn't expecting such a profound response. "What do you mean?" she asked. "About us all needing help?"

Joe paused, looking off into the distance like someone who'd seen a lot. "Everyone's got their struggles," he said. "Some of us just have battles that are easier to see."

Maggie thought about that for a minute. "I've never looked at it that way."

With a tired but kind smile, Joe explained how he'd lost his job, and after that, everything spiraled. "It's hard to get back up once you're down."

Maggie, determined, asked, "Is there anything I can do to help you get back on your feet?"

Joe smiled. "You're already doing it. Listening and caring. That matters more than you think."

Over the next few weeks, Maggie didn't just listen, she took action. She helped connect Joe to resources at the shelter and even found him a job program. With time, Joe regained his confidence and saved enough money to rent an apartment. As he stood in his new place, he thanked Maggie for restoring his hope. He also realized how powerful helping others really is and told her he planned to give back by volunteering at the shelter.

And there you have it. Humility, gratitude, and a little help from others can turn things around in ways you never expect.

AFFIRMATION

I'm the master of my shift!

I share kindness and appreciate the kindness and generosity of others.

WEEK NINE

DAY 3

Unveiling Your True Self

What do you appreciate in your life and what do you need help with?

_____
_____
_____
_____
_____
_____
_____
_____
_____
_____
_____
_____
_____
_____
_____
_____

Every action in our lives touches on some chord that will vibrate in eternity.
– Edwin Hubbel Chapin

WEEK NINE

Humility

DAY 4

Respect for Others

Humble people have a way of treating everyone they meet with respect, regardless of their background, beliefs, or social status. They recognize that every person has inherent worth, and they approach others with a sense of equality and kindness. It's not about making grand gestures or seeking praise; it's about honoring the dignity of others in their everyday interactions.

Here's the thing: being humble means understanding that we all share this world and no one is better or more deserving based on superficial things like social status, wealth, or appearance. Humility teaches us to treat the janitor the same way we treat the CEO—to look beyond external labels and value the person inside. That's real respect.

Now, imagine you're on a packed flight, and a well-to-do passenger throws a fit because they've been seated next to someone they believe is beneath them. How would you handle that situation?

This exact scenario played out on a flight from Johannesburg. A middle-aged woman was horrified to find herself seated next to an African man and demanded to be moved. The flight attendant, keeping her cool, offered to check for other available seats in business or first class. The woman, full of arrogance, waited impatiently, while other passengers watched the scene unfold.

When the flight attendant returned, she delivered the most unexpected twist. "I found a seat in first class," she said with a smile, before turning to the man. "Sir, if you would kindly gather your things, we've upgraded you to first class."

The rest of the passengers broke into applause as the man, who had quietly endured the insult, was given the respect and dignity he deserved. The flight attendant's graceful handling of the situation not only highlighted the injustice but also demonstrated how humility can be paired with action to put respect front and center.

This story reminds us that humility isn't just about staying quiet, it's about standing up for what's right while treating others with fairness and respect. True humility respects others, no matter who they are, and makes the world a kinder place in the process.

AFFIRMATION

I'm the master of my shift!

I respect and appreciate the diversity of the human race.

WEEK NINE

DAY 4

Unveiling Your True Self

In what ways do you demonstrate respect for others?

Every object, every being, is a jar of delight. Be a connoisseur.
– Rumi

WEEK NINE

Humility

DAY 5

Community Service

The transformative power of community service lies in its ability to change lives and reshape communities. For you, the act of serving others can be life-changing, instilling a sense of purpose and fulfillment. For your community, the collective efforts of volunteers can lead to significant improvements in quality of life and social well-being.

Studies show that humility often manifests as a willingness to serve others and contribute to the greater good of society. Volunteers report that prioritizing the needs of others above their own increases their happiness, enriches their life, and gives them a sense of purpose and belonging. Most importantly, volunteering will awaken joy within your soul and those you serve.

Since the premise of this 15-week program is to shift your outlook on life so you can be happier and achieve your dreams, volunteering is an important component in helping you achieve those goals. Volunteering exposes you to diverse perspectives and experiences, deepens your understanding of the struggles and triumphs of others, increases your self-esteem, and generally leads to a more fulfilling life.

Community service can also give you valuable skills and experiences that will enhance your career. You will develop leadership, teamwork, and problem-solving abilities that are highly sought after in the job market. Additionally, community service provides networking opportunities and connects you with like-minded people and potential mentors that can open doors to new career paths and professional growth.

The benefits to your community are both immediate and long-lasting. On an immediate level, community service addresses pressing needs, such as providing food, shelter, education, or healthcare to those in need. This creates a safety net for vulnerable populations and ensures that basic needs are met and dignity is preserved. In the long term, community service fosters social cohesion and resilience, builds trust and collaboration among community members, strengthens social bonds, all of which create a supportive and connected community environment.

I'm the master of my shift!

AFFIRMATION

I find joy and fulfillment in helping others.

WEEK NINE

DAY 5

Unveiling Your True Self

In what ways has community service enriched your life?

Help others achieve their dreams and you will achieve yours.
– Les Brown

WEEK NINE

Humility

DAY 6

Adaptability

Adaptability is all about being open to learning and rolling with the punches when life throws you a curveball. Humble people know that they don't have all the answers, and they're willing to adapt and grow from whatever experiences come their way. Take Brandi, for example.

Brandi was a graphic designer who loved her routines—she had her favorite coffee shop, her cozy evenings at home, and a pretty predictable day-to-day life. Everything was running smoothly until one chilly autumn morning, when her world turned upside down. Her boss, Mr. Harris, called an emergency meeting. "The company's closing down due to financial trouble. I'm really sorry," he announced, leaving the room in stunned silence.

Brandi felt her heart sink. Her job wasn't just a paycheck; it was her sense of identity. For days, she frantically sent out job applications, waiting for a response that never came. As the rejection letters piled up, so did her anxiety.

Then, one evening, her friend Jake called with a lead. A tech startup was hiring, though the role involved much more than just graphic design. Hesitant but desperate, Brandi took the job. What followed was a whirlwind. Learning new software, a chaotic schedule, and tasks that stretched her beyond her usual skill set left her feeling out of her depth. She often found herself working late, struggling to keep up.

One night, as Brandi wrestled with yet another tough project, the CEO, Lisa, approached her. "Brandi, I know this is a big shift for you, but I see potential. We need your creativity. Don't be afraid to step outside your comfort zone."

That was the wake-up call Brandi needed. She realized that holding onto her old routine was holding her back. Determined to adapt, she started sharing ideas, learning from her team, and embracing the new pace of things. Slowly, she found joy in the chaos and started thriving in the startup's energetic environment.

Brandi's story is proof that adaptability isn't just about surviving change; it's about growing through it. By stepping out of her comfort zone, Brandi turned uncertainty into opportunity, showing that true humility lies in being willing to grow, no matter where life takes you.

I'm the master of my shift!

AFFIRMATION

I am grateful for the lessons I learn from challenges and setbacks.

WEEK NINE — DAY 6

Unveiling Your True Self

What have you learned about yourself when faced with a life-changing event?

_____
_____
_____
_____
_____
_____
_____
_____
_____
_____
_____
_____
_____
_____

I am not a product of my circumstances. I am a product of my decisions.
— Stephen R. Covey

WEEK NINE

Humility

DAY 7

Self-Reflection

Humble people are all about checking in with themselves and taking the time to reflect on their thoughts, actions, and what really motivates them. They know that personal growth doesn't just happen overnight, and they're always striving to become better versions of themselves. It's not about being perfect but about being open to self-improvement and staying grounded in humility.

Take Alex, for example. A well-liked high school teacher, always upbeat, always involved in the community, and always there to lend a helping hand. From the outside, everything seemed great, but deep down, Alex felt a nagging dissatisfaction. He couldn't quite figure out why, but he knew something wasn't right.

One evening, after a rough day at work, he decided to clear his head with a walk along the river. As he strolled, he spotted an old bench he had passed countless times but never really noticed. Feeling the need to pause, he sat down, letting the cool breeze wash over him, and for the first time in ages, he gazed at the river and allowed himself to just think.

"What am I doing?" he asked himself. "Why am I feeling this way?"

These questions stuck with him. So the next day, Alex turned inward for answers. He bought a journal and started a daily practice sitting on his bench and writing down his thoughts and feelings. At first, the process felt awkward. He wasn't used to digging so deep into his inner world. But as the weeks went by, he started to see the benefits. He recognized patterns in his behavior—like how he always kept busy to avoid dealing with deeper issues like his fear of failure and his need for validation.

One evening, as he took his seat by the river, he thought about how much self-reflection had opened his eyes to things he'd been avoiding for years. It helped him slow down, reframe his thoughts, and discover more about who he really was and what he wanted out of life. He knew that self-reflection was now a lifelong habit that would keep guiding him on his journey to growth and fulfillment.

I'm the master of my shift!

AFFIRMATION

I trust my intuition and inner guidance.

WEEK NINE

DAY 7

Unveiling Your True Self

What insights have you gained from self-reflection?

Life is a long lesson in humility.
– James M. Barrie

Week 10

Integrity

The Shift Code Daily Routine Checklist

WEEK TEN | *Integrity*	Day 1	Day 2	Day 3	Day 4	Day 5	Day 6	Day 7
In the Morning:							
I began my day by smiling and saying, "I am grateful for this day and the positive shift I'm creating in my life!"							
I read the daily action plan in my workbook.							
I made note of the focus of my affirmation(s) and self-talk for the day.							
I identified one or more action steps for the day.							
During the Day:							
I repeated my affirmation(s) and consciously reprogrammed my chatter brain's self-talk.							
I reflected on the Mindful Brain Fuel daily inspiration and quote of the day.							
I initiated my action step(s) for today.							
I exercised.							
In the Evening:							
I checked off the items I completed on the daily plan.							
I answered the self-reflection question.							
I jotted down my thoughts about my journey.							
I ended my day by smiling and saying, "I am grateful for this day and the positive shift I created in my life today!"							
Bonus Activities:							
I meditated.							
I completed a random act of kindness.							
I paid it forward.							
I read an inspirational book.							
I experienced AWE!							
Other: _____							

WEEK TEN

Integrity

DAY 1

Honesty

Integrity is an overarching virtue that encompasses many other values, ethical principles, behaviors, and attitudes including, but not limited to, being honest, trustworthy, morally courageous, accountable, fair, loyal, and humble. Cultivating these qualities and doing the right thing in alignment with your core values will help you be seen and respected as a person with integrity.

As we think about honesty as a component of integrity, let's begin with being truthful, meaning, you consistently tell the truth, you're not deceitful, and you're straightforward and sincere in your communication with others. An example would be telling someone that their racist joke was unacceptable, or speaking up in a meeting or social situation when someone makes an offensive comment. It takes moral courage to stand up for what's right and you may risk disapproval from others in doing so, but that's what makes cultivating integrity so difficult.

What if you and a colleague made a mistake on a project at work that could cost your company a huge amount of money? Your colleague suggests covering it up to avoid repercussions, arguing that no one would find out. You are tempted to follow that advice and have several sleepless nights stewing about doing the right thing or going with the flow.

In the end, your true character shines through and you decide to act in alignment with your core values—your honesty and integrity win. You confess the error to your boss and provide a detailed report of the mistake and proposed solutions to mitigate the impact. This results in you having peace of mind, being commended for your honesty, earning the respect of your boss and colleagues, and ultimately receiving a promotion.

Bottom line—honest people admit their mistakes and provide accurate information even when it's difficult, and they are truthful and transparent in what they say.

I'm the master of my shift!

AFFIRMATION

I lead by example, demonstrating honesty and integrity in all that I do.

WEEK TEN — **DAY 1**

Unveiling Your True Self

How do you handle situations where being honest might have negative consequences?

_____
_____
_____
_____
_____
_____
_____
_____
_____
_____
_____
_____
_____
_____
_____

A lie gets halfway around the world before the truth has a chance to get its pants on.
—Winston Churchill

WEEK TEN

Integrity

DAY 2

Trustworthy

Honesty and trustworthiness are closely related concepts that are essential for building strong, meaningful personal and professional relationships. Honest people are considered trustworthy when they are reliable and consistent in fulfilling their commitments, meeting deadlines, and keeping their promises. In other words, their behavior is consistent and predictable over time, and that builds confidence and trust in their capabilities.

In the example given yesterday about honesty, your colleague that wanted to cover up the mistake would be branded untrustworthy, definitely not something that's going to help them get ahead professionally. In addition, if they are willing to cover up a mistake in business, it brings into question how much they can be trusted in personal relationships.

What if one of your friends at work confided in you about making a significant change in their life, such as leaving their high-paying corporate job to start a nonprofit for underprivileged children? They ask you to not share their plans with anyone else until they have everything set.

You promise to keep the secret, but over the next few weeks, find it increasingly difficult to maintain your vow of silence. Friends and colleagues at work have noticed a change in your friend's behavior at work as well as at social settings and they keep asking you for information. Even your boss asked you about your friend's disengagement at work. You honor your promise and do not divulge your friend's plan.

Finally, the day arrives when your friend announces her plan and shares her vision with your circle of friends and colleagues. She thanks you for being such a steadfast confidante and in that moment, you realize that this wasn't just about withholding information; it was about supporting your friend's journey and respecting her wishes. By keeping her confidence, you played a crucial role in helping your friend take a brave step forward.

Through this experience your reputation for being a trustworthy person blossoms. Colleagues and friends confide in you because they know you'll follow through on your promises and maintain confidentiality.

I'm the master of my shift!

AFFIRMATION

I build trust through my consistent and ethical behavior.

WEEK TEN

DAY 2

Unveiling Your True Self

Have there been instances where you failed to be trustworthy? What were the consequences, and how did you address them?

_____
_____
_____
_____
_____
_____
_____
_____
_____
_____
_____
_____
_____
_____
_____

*Whoever is careless with the truth in small matters
cannot be trusted in important affairs.*
– Albert Einstein

WEEK TEN

Integrity

DAY 3

Ethics

For centuries, philosophers have generated theories for distinguishing right from wrong as well as guidelines for how to live and act ethically. These philosophical discussions have led to the study of ethics from many perspectives and deal with concepts such as responsibility, rights, and virtues. Ethics plays a crucial role in society by helping individuals and groups make decisions that contribute to the greater good, maintain social order, and foster trust and cooperation. Ethical questions arise in all facets of our personal and professional lives.

Although acting ethically may not always be top of mind in our daily decisions, ethics is a foundational element that guides us to make decisions in alignment with values such as honesty, fairness, justice, and respect for others. On the world stage, ethics contributes to the greater good, helps maintain social order, and fosters trust and cooperation. Choosing to act ethically offers us the opportunity to explore questions like "What should I do?" and "What are my obligations to others in terms of right versus wrong, good versus bad, and fair versus unfair?"

The following steps in how to make ethical decisions are an excerpt from the framework for ethical decision making at the Markkula Center for Applied Ethics at Santa Clara University. The complete framework is online at https://www.scu.edu/ethics/ethics-resources/a-framework-for-ethical-decision-making/.

1) Identify the Ethical Issues
2) Get the Facts
3) Evaluate Alternative Actions
4) Choose an Option for Action and Test It
5) Implement Your Decision and Reflect on the Outcome

Studying ethics can give you deep insights into what people do and why they do it and can help you define your ethical boundaries so your decisions are aligned with your personal code of conduct. Your ethical standards not only define how you interact personally and professionally, but with animals, everything on our planet and beyond. As you apply your ethical code to real life, your courage, compassion, wisdom, and kindness will be revealed. Others will be inclined to follow your lead as they see you living a fulfilling life with a purpose greater than yourself. When you're motivated by the right principles, you will act ethically.

I'm the master of my shift!

AFFIRMATION

Acting ethically is integral to my character and values.

WEEK TEN

DAY 3

Unveiling Your True Self

What does ethics mean to you?

_____
_____
_____
_____
_____
_____
_____
_____
_____
_____
_____
_____
_____
_____
_____

*Like birds, ethical issues are everywhere...often difficult to spot,
but noticed by those in search of them.
– Markkula Center for Applied Ethics*

WEEK TEN

Integrity

DAY 4

Competence

Competence refers to the knowledge, skills, and expertise needed to fulfill responsibilities effectively. Being recognized as a competent person enhances your trustworthiness among peers and can lead to more influential positions throughout your life. Although we typically think of competence in relation to job skills, it certainly applies to all aspects of our lives and is more than just a skill set. Your competence grows in many ways every day, as a friend, family member, coach, mentor, student, or in social situations.

Mastering the art of being competent, as with all the concepts presented in this program, are a lifelong pursuit that involves constant growth and adaptation. It's about striving to do your best in every situation while also recognizing that perfection is not the goal—continuous improvement is. Here are a few tips:

- Trust in your abilities, but also recognize when you need help or advice.
- Regularly ask for constructive feedback to help you grow.
- Stay curious and learn new things.
- Be flexible and adapt as new information or circumstances arise.
- Be a good listener and pay attention to what others are saying.
- Be organized and manage your time effectively.
- Think outside the box and develop innovative solutions.
- Stay humble, build relationships, be honest, and be accountable.

Twice in my career, I accepted jobs that were out of my comfort zone and required skills and knowledge beyond my current abilities. In both cases, I was passionate about the jobs and that passion drove me to study and gain the expertise necessary to excel. It was scary for a while as I learned what these positions entailed, but I persevered, asked for help, got a mentor, and ultimately gained the knowledge that eventually thrust me into positions with more responsibility and authority.

I'm the master of my shift!

AFFIRMATION

My competence and integrity work together to create success.

WEEK TEN

DAY 4

Unveiling Your True Self

In what areas do you need to expand your competence and what's your plan for becoming more competent?

_____

_____

_____

_____

_____

_____

_____

_____

_____

_____

_____

_____

_____

_____

_____

_____

Bragging about yourself violates norms of modesty and politeness—and if you were really competent, your work would speak for itself.
– Adam Grant

WEEK TEN

Integrity

DAY 5

Transparency

Being open and transparent personally and professionally builds trust, and trust breeds loyalty, credibility, and respect. Let's say you decide to live in a glass house. Everyone walking by can see you working at your desk, cooking in the kitchen, or relaxing in your favorite chair reading a book or watching TV. You live openly and hide nothing. People are fascinated and ask how you can live like that. You simply say, "I have nothing to hide. What you see is who I am."

As people get to know you better, they understand that you value authenticity and transparency. Your open about your thoughts and feelings. When you're happy, they see your joy. When you're sad, they see your tears. And, if you make a mistake, you freely admit and learn from it. You're openness encourages them to take down barriers and share more of themselves. Your honesty and kindness spreads, and people learn that being open and transparent doesn't mean being vulnerable or exposed. It means being true to oneself and others.

In your professional life, your openness and transparency fosters understanding, reduces uncertainty, and builds trust through increased clarity and communication. Colleagues respect your willingness to share information and know they can trust your intentions and decisions.

A lack of trust is any organization's biggest enemy. It can take years for leaders to develop the trust of employees and customers, but only moments to lose it.

Without trust

- influence is destroyed;
- leaders lose credibility; and
- organizations lose productivity, relationships, reputation, talent, loyalty, creativity, morale, revenue, and results.

Trust, not money, is the currency of business.

With trust, organizations

- find and close gaps in organizational efficiency and effectiveness;
- cultivate support to develop a clear path forward; and
- gain credibility and respect.

I'm the master of my shift!

AFFIRMATION

I value transparency and communicate openly and honestly.

WEEK TEN — **DAY 5**

Unveiling Your True Self

How would your life change if you were more open and transparent?

_____

_____

_____

_____

_____

_____

_____

_____

_____

_____

_____

_____

_____

_____

Being truthful and open creates trust. A lack of transparency results in distrust and a deep sense of insecurity.
— **Dalai Lama**

WEEK TEN

Integrity

DAY 6

Loyalty

Loyalty is a strong feeling of allegiance, commitment, and support toward someone or something. It involves a steadfast devotion and trust, often characterized by reliability and a willingness to stand by a person, cause, or organization even in difficult times. Loyalty can manifest in various forms, such as in relationships, friendships, employment, and ideologies, and is often seen as a core value that strengthens bonds and fosters trustworthiness. However, balancing loyalty with integrity can be challenging. The Theranos story is a powerful example of the conflict between loyalty and integrity.

Founded in 2003 by Elizabeth Holmes, the company claimed to revolutionize blood testing with a single drop of blood. Holmes's vision captivated investors and employees, quickly raising millions of dollars and securing high-profile partnerships.

However, behind the scenes, Theranos's technology was deeply flawed, often producing inaccurate results. Despite this, Holmes and her executives continued to deceive investors and hide the truth.

Employees at Theranos faced a moral dilemma, torn between their loyalty to the company and their commitment to integrity. One notable figure, Tyler Shultz, the grandson of board member George Shultz (former US Secretary of State), discovered the company's unethical practices. Tyler chose to prioritize his integrity over his loyalty to the company and became a whistleblower, exposing the truth at great personal cost.

Tyler's actions were crucial in revealing Theranos's fraud, leading to the company's downfall and sparking a broader conversation about ethics in the tech and healthcare industries. The Theranos story highlights the importance of balancing loyalty with integrity, particularly in environments where the pressure to conform can be overwhelming. It shows that while loyalty is a valuable trait, it should never come at the expense of ethical principles. Tyler Shultz's actions remind us that true loyalty to others—and to oneself—sometimes means speaking out and doing what's right, even when it's difficult.

I'm the master of my shift!

AFFIRMATION

Loyalty and integrity are the foundations of my relationships.

WEEK TEN — DAY 6

Unveiling Your True Self

How do you balance loyalty with personal integrity? What if being loyal conflicts with your values or well-being? How do you decide when to stand by someone or something and when to step back?

Faithless is he that says farewell when the road darkens.
– J.R.R. Tolkien

WEEK TEN

Integrity

DAY 7

Accountability

Accountability means taking ownership of our actions, decisions, and outcomes by demonstrating a commitment to ethical conduct, reliability, and integrity. When you're accountable, you acknowledge when you've made a mistake, take responsibility for your actions, and actively work to resolve any issues that arise. The following examples demonstrate accountability and acting ethically. Think about how you may have handled a similar situation in the past or how you would handle it today.

PERSONAL SCENARIOS

- You accidentally break a friend's item; you immediately apologize and offer to replace or repair it.

- You promise to help a friend move; you show up on time and help as much as possible.

- You inadvertently hurt someone's feelings, you apologize sincerely and take actions to repair the relationship.

- You see a task or chore that needs to be done, like cleaning up a shared space; you do it without waiting for someone else to take responsibility.

- You're running late for an appointment or meeting; you call the other person and let them know you're on your way.

WORK SCENARIOS

- You encounter challenges or delays in your work; you communicate these issues to your team or manager as soon as possible, providing updates on how you're addressing them.

- You make an error in a report or presentation; you promptly correct it and inform your supervisor or colleagues about the mistake.

- You receive constructive criticism from a manager or colleague; you listen without becoming defensive, reflect on the feedback, and make improvements based on it.

- Your actions cause a problem for a client or team; you take steps to rectify the situation, such as offering a solution or compensation.

- A project you led doesn't meet expectations; you accept the responsibility for the outcome and work to improve future performance.

I'm the master of my shift!

AFFIRMATION

I am accountable for acting with integrity and in alignment with my core values.

WEEK TEN — — — — — — — — — — — **DAY 7**

Unveiling Your True Self

What does being accountable mean to you personally and professionally?

_____
_____
_____
_____
_____
_____
_____
_____
_____
_____
_____
_____
_____
_____
_____
_____

Trust, honesty, humility, transparency and accountability are the building blocks of a positive reputation. Trust is the foundation of any relationship.
– Mike Paul

WEEK 11

EMOTIONAL INTELLIGENCE

The Shift Code Daily Routine Checklist

WEEK ELEVEN | *Emotional Intelligence*	Day 1	Day 2	Day 3	Day 4	Day 5	Day 6	Day 7
In the Morning:							
I began my day by smiling and saying, "I am grateful for this day and the positive shift I'm creating in my life!"							
I read the daily action plan in my workbook.							
I made note of the focus of my affirmation(s) and self-talk for the day.							
I identified one or more action steps for the day.							
During the Day:							
I repeated my affirmation(s) and consciously reprogrammed my chatter brain's self-talk.							
I reflected on the Mindful Brain Fuel daily inspiration and quote of the day.							
I initiated my action step(s) for today.							
I exercised.							
In the Evening:							
I checked off the items I completed on the daily plan.							
I answered the self-reflection question.							
I jotted down my thoughts about my journey.							
I ended my day by smiling and saying, "I am grateful for this day and the positive shift I created in my life today!"							
Bonus Activities:							
I meditated.							
I completed a random act of kindness.							
I paid it forward.							
I read an inspirational book.							
I experienced AWE!							
Other: _____							

WEEK ELEVEN

Emotional Intelligence

DAY 1

Inner Consciousness

Emotional intelligence is like having magical abilities that help you master your own emotions and understand the emotional weather patterns swirling around your interactions with others. Remember back in Week Two, Day 1, Wake Up! when I asked you to pay attention to your thoughts, feelings, and behaviors? That was your first step in developing your inner consciousness. Now that you're further along in tuning into your own emotional cues, you're also improving your ability to read cues from others, which helps you better understand their feelings. These are important steps along your path to becoming emotionally intelligent.

We all like to be around emotionally intelligent people because they make us feel appreciated and valued. Their innate sense of self-awareness, empathy, and humbleness paired with excellent communication and conflict management skills facilitates their ability to listen and process not only what they have heard, but also what they observed in our body language before they speak or act. Their interactions with us seem effortless, and they give the illusion of having superpowers when it comes to understanding where we are coming from and how to best relate to us.

For those of you who are interested in a deeper understanding of your emotional intelligence, I suggest taking the IHHP (Institute for Health and Human Potential) EI360™ Assessment. The assessment is based on neuroscience research and provides a report to your answers across eleven emotional intelligence competencies. There is a cost associated with the assessment and this is not a paid advertisement. I mention it only because I have taken the assessment and found it to be informative and useful in my own personal development. https://www.ihhp.com/

If you would like to see how well you can read the emotions behind facial expressions, take the free emotional intelligence quiz on the Greater Good Science Center website (https://greatergood.berkeley.edu/quizzes/ei_quiz). This quiz dives into deciphering facial features when people express various emotions such as happiness, anger, disgust, and more. The Greater Good Science Center studies the psychology, sociology, and neuroscience of well-being, and teaches skills that foster a thriving, resilient, and compassionate society.

I'm the master of my shift!

AFFIRMATION

I am more emotionally intelligent every day.

WEEK ELEVEN — DAY 1

Unveiling Your True Self

How does your emotional intelligence vary in different settings, e.g., work, home, social situations? What areas need improvement?

_____

_____

_____

_____

_____

_____

_____

_____

_____

_____

_____

_____

_____

_____

_____

To know thyself is the beginning of wisdom.
– Socrates

WEEK ELEVEN

Emotional Intelligence

DAY 2

Body Language

Body language refers to the physical gestures we use consciously and unconsciously when we speak. These nonverbal signals convey additional information about our feelings and emotions and according to scientists, may account for 60 to 65% of all our communication. If you took the quiz on the Greater Good Science Center website mentioned in the Inner Consciousness discussion yesterday, you already understand more about the meaning of facial and eye expressions; however, body language also includes other gestures, posture, body movements, and personal space.

I am including body language in this section to help you become more aware of how you communicate through your facial expressions and body movements. As you observe yourself, you may become more aware of others as well, but keep in mind that thoroughly understanding body language is an art that takes years of training and practice. Once you begin to learn various nonverbal signals it may be tempting to pick them apart one by one. So remember it's important to look at them as a whole in relation to the words being spoken and the context of the specific situation.

The best way to read someone's body language is to pay attention. First tune into your physical movements to learn how you combine your verbal and nonverbal cues in different contexts, (i.e., social versus professional settings). Then, observe others to begin understanding how their body language relates to what they are saying. There are way too many cues to articulate here, but the following hints are a good place to start:

- While you say that you are feeling fine, the look on your face may tell people otherwise.

- The expression on your face can determine if you can be trusted or believed.

- One study found that the most trustworthy facial expression involves a slight raise of the eyebrows and a slight smile. It also conveys friendliness and confidence.

- People with smiling, joyful expressions are perceived as being more intelligent than those with angry expressions.

- Gestures are another significant form of nonverbal communication, but they can also be influenced by culture. For instance, giving a thumbs-up or peace sign in another country may have a completely different meaning than it does in the United States.

There's no one-size-fits-all approach to interpreting nonverbal cues. However, increasing awareness of your own body language should help you become a better communicator.

AFFIRMATION

I'm the master of my shift!

I practice mindful body language to create positive interactions with others.

WEEK ELEVEN

DAY 2

Unveiling Your True Self

How does your body language affect the effectiveness of your communication?

_____

_____

_____

_____

_____

_____

_____

_____

_____

_____

_____

_____

_____

_____

_____

The most important thing in communication is hearing what isn't said.
– Peter Drucker

WEEK ELEVEN

Emotional Intelligence

DAY 3

Cerebral Blueprint

I believe that the more we understand ourselves, the better we can communicate with others, and that's why I'm including resources throughout this program that can help you learn and grow. Among the many personal development and personality assessments available, the one I have found the most helpful is Emergenetics (https://emergenetics.com). It's science-based, easy to understand, and applicable in personal and professional settings.

Emergenetics organizes our thinking preferences into four categories: Conceptual, Social, Analytical, and Structural. Now you may immediately put yourself in one or more of those categories, but I need to emphasize that even though we all have a preferred style, we also have the capability to use any of these styles at any time depending on the situation. To give you an idea of how each style approaches life, let's take a look at how four friends, each with a unique style, prefer to plan a vacation.

Ginny, the conceptual dreamer of the group, leans back in her chair, eyes twinkling with possibilities. Her imagination explodes with grand ideas thinking of experience that would transcend the ordinary and explore uncharted territories, much like her approach to life. She shared her vision with her friends by painting imaginary scenes in the air. She grabs her bag and heads for the airport.

Veronica, the group's analytical thinker, loves the idea but needs more data. She volunteered to develop a budget and analyze any potential risks. She prepared categorized lists for the exact time required for each destination, best season to visit, health advisories, travel restrictions, and so on.

Oliver, the structural thinker, is practical and needs order and precision. He said he would outline a detailed schedule—day by day, hour by hour—and make Plans A, B, and C outlining every contingency he could think of. He would create a checklist, map out routes, schedule transportation, lodging, and activities. His methodical approach helps the trip run smoothly but leaves out any room for spontaneity.

Finally, Mark, the social thinker, chimed in with his perspective that what matters most is the company we keep and the experiences we share. He prefers a destination where they can interact with locals, make new friends, and even participate in community projects. His approach emphasized the importance of relationships and the emotional richness of the experience, focusing on how the trip could deepen their bonds.

I'm the master of my shift!

AFFIRMATION

I celebrate diversity in thought, knowing it enriches every conversation.

WEEK ELEVEN

DAY 3

Unveiling Your True Self

Which of these thinking styles do you think you are and why? How would the four styles complement one another as a team?

_____
_____
_____
_____
_____
_____
_____
_____
_____
_____
_____
_____
_____
_____
_____

If everyone is thinking alike, then somebody isn't thinking.
– George S. Patton

WEEK ELEVEN

Emotional Intelligence

DAY 4

Behavioral Blueprint

As with the thinking preferences mentioned yesterday, we all have behavioral preferences as well. Again, using the Emergenetics model, let's explore three behavioral attributes—Expressiveness, Assertiveness, and Flexibility. Everyone has all three of these and uses each one to a greater or lesser degree depending on the situation. Let's take a brief look at examples of a few of the characteristics within each attribute.

Expressiveness ranges from
- quiet to outgoing
- calm to lively
- introverted to extroverted

Assertiveness ranges from
- peacekeeper to determined
- accepting to telling
- amiable to forceful

Flexibility ranges from
- focused to seeing many options
- firm to easy going
- impatient with change to changeable.

I believe it's critical for your growth as a communicator to understand where your comfort zone falls within these ranges and in what situations you need to learn to slide from one end of the spectrum toward the other. For instance, let's say you're a naturally quiet, introverted person but you have to make an important presentation to a large audience. To engage your audience, this means you have to move to the outgoing, lively, more extroverted side of the spectrum. Your presentation goes well and you receive compliments and accolades for your work, but it comes at a cost. Because you were out of your natural comfort zone, you expended a lot more energy during the presentation, and it exhausted you. Now you need some quiet time to recover.

If you want to know your thinking and behavioral preferences, you'll need to take the online Emergenetics assessment. There is a cost associated with the assessment and, as with all the companies I mention, I do not receive any compensation. I include them because they are additional resources that can enrich your personal development journey.

I'm the master of my shift!

AFFIRMATION

I understand how my behavior influences how others perceive me.

WEEK ELEVEN

DAY 4

Unveiling Your True Self

In what personal and professional situations do you need to be more or less expressive, assertive, or flexible?

Behavior is the mirror in which everyone shows their image.
– Johann von Goethe

WEEK ELEVEN

Emotional Intelligence

DAY 5

Communication

Communication is a vital component of being emotionally intelligent and while we may think it's easy—you talk, I listen; I talk, you listen—it's really much more complex. As mentioned in previous brain fuel segments this week, there are verbal and nonverbal cues, different thinking styles that filter how we give and receive information, and different settings in our personal and professional lives that activate behaviors and emotions that can color conversations. That's a lot to take in so it's easy to see how miscommunication happens.

To be a good communicator, you need to prepare and present your ideas in a clear, logical, and succinct manner. One of the easiest ways to get folks aligned is to define the who, what, why, where, when, and how. Some people have great ideas but have trouble articulating them in a way that others understand. Others may be so wordy that they lose their audience in minutia. If people don't understand your vision, they won't get on board to support you.

I suggest you adopt an assertive style, sharing your thoughts and ideas confidently but always remaining respectful and polite. Speak with a clear friendly voice, make eye contact, be aware of your body language, and make others feel comfortable expressing their ideas in an open and collaborative space.

Know your audience. Whether you're making a group presentation or having a one-on-one conversation, try organizing your ideas in ways that appeal to each Emergenetics thinking preference:

- Conceptual
  Provide overview/summary, visualize big picture, use pictures and color

- Social
  Use stories, eye contact, establish rapport, relate to people

- Analytical
  Provide data, numbers, establish credibility

- Structural
  Provide an agenda, details, steps/bullet points, action plan

Poor communicators interrupt people while they're speaking, invade personal space, present an overbearing posture, use aggressive gestures, mutter, use sarcasm, give the silent treatment, or maintain intense intimidating eye contact.

Good communicators are good listeners and encourage others to share their ideas. They exercise emotional intelligence, and are direct (assertive), without being aggressive, open to feedback, authentic, calm, friendly, and professional.

AFFIRMATION

I'm the master of my shift!

I am dedicated to being a good listener and improving my communication skills.

WEEK ELEVEN

DAY 5

Unveiling Your True Self

How will you use emotional intelligence to adapt your messages to people that process information differently than you do?

To effectively communicate, we must realize that we are all different in the way we perceive the world and use this understanding as a guide to our communication with others.
– Tony Robbins

WEEK ELEVEN

Emotional Intelligence

DAY 6

Tact

Your ability to communicate with tact and diplomacy can make or break your personal and professional relationships. Although being tactful and diplomatic comes naturally to some people, for most of us, it's a lifelong pursuit. Tact and diplomacy aren't merely optional soft skills; they are fundamental components of emotional intelligence that will help you navigate complex social landscapes, manage conflicts with grace, and lead with empathy and understanding. In a world where effective communication and collaboration are key to achieving personal and professional goals, the value of tact and diplomacy cannot be overstated.

Tact is your ability to handle delicate or sensitive situations with sensitivity and care. It involves the thoughtful selection of words, tone, and timing to convey messages in a way that minimizes potential conflict or offense. Tact requires an acute awareness of both verbal and nonverbal cues, as well as an understanding of the emotional states of others.

In a professional setting, tact is particularly important when delivering feedback, addressing mistakes, or managing conflicts. For example, a manager who criticizes an employee's performance without tact may inadvertently demoralize the individual, leading to decreased productivity and engagement. Conversely, a tactful approach—acknowledging the employee's efforts, highlighting areas for improvement in a constructive manner, and offering support—can foster a positive outcome, where the employee feels valued and motivated to improve.

Tact is also vital in multicultural environments, where differences in communication styles, cultural norms, and expectations can lead to misunderstandings. A tactful individual can navigate these differences by showing respect for diverse perspectives, adapting their communication style, and finding common ground. This ability to bridge cultural gaps not only enhances collaboration but also promotes inclusivity and mutual respect.

I'm the master of my shift!

AFFIRMATION

I am tactful.

WEEK ELEVEN — DAY 6

Unveiling Your True Self

How do you use tact to build trust and rapport with others?

_____
_____
_____
_____
_____
_____
_____
_____
_____
_____
_____
_____
_____
_____

Tact is the art of making a point without making an enemy.
— Isaac Newton

WEEK ELEVEN

Emotional Intelligence

DAY 7

Diplomacy

Diplomacy is the art of strategic communication where you skillfully balance relationships and interests to achieve favorable outcomes. It's particularly crucial in roles where the ability to build alliances, mediate disputes, and guide teams toward shared goals is essential. Diplomatic people balance assertiveness with empathy, ensuring that their own objectives are met without alienating or antagonizing others.

Effective diplomacy requires a deep understanding of power dynamics, as well as the ability to anticipate and respond to the needs and concerns of others. Being diplomatic in your personal relationships as well as in professional settings can help you align different interests, foster collaboration, and resolve conflicts in a way that preserves relationships and maintains interpersonal or organizational harmony. When you're tactful and diplomatic, you're more likely to achieve win-win outcomes and lay the foundation for long-term partnerships and trust.

Let's look at the different approaches taken by two colleagues who work in the same department at a marketing firm. Emily is known for her high emotional intelligence, while Jake struggles in this area.

Emily has a unique ability to connect with others. She senses when someone is upset, even if they're trying to hide it. One day, their team faced a tight deadline and she noticed that Sarah, a junior team member, seemed particularly anxious and the pressure was getting to her. Instead of brushing off Sarah's anxiety, Emily took a moment to pull her aside, asked how she was doing, and offered to help.

Jake, on the other hand, was the opposite. He is technically skilled and confident in his abilities but lacks emotional awareness. The day of the deadline he was focused solely on his tasks, oblivious to the mood around him. When Sarah approached him to ask for help, he barely noticed her and told her to just figure it out—he didn't have time to babysit people.

Emily's positive influence kept Sarah and the team motivated, while Jake's lack of empathy and harshness created an undercurrent of unease. He was clueless to the impact he had on the team and the negative feelings he had fostered. In the end, Emily's empathy and emotional intelligence not only made her a better colleague but also paved the way for her success, while Jake's inability to connect with others isolated him and limited his potential.

I'm the master of my shift!

AFFIRMATION

I am diplomatic.

WEEK ELEVEN — DAY 7

Unveiling Your True Self

Think of someone you respect for their tact and diplomacy. What behaviors and communication skills do they exhibit that you would like to emulate?

_____
_____
_____
_____
_____
_____
_____
_____
_____
_____
_____
_____
_____
_____

Diplomacy is the art of letting somebody else have your way.
– David Frost

Week 12

Spirituality

The Shift Code Daily Routine Checklist

WEEK TWELVE | *Spirituality*	Day 1	Day 2	Day 3	Day 4	Day 5	Day 6	Day 7
In the Morning:							
I began my day by smiling and saying, "I am grateful for this day and the positive shift I'm creating in my life!"							
I read the daily action plan in my workbook.							
I made note of the focus of my affirmation(s) and self-talk for the day.							
I identified one or more action steps for the day.							
During the Day:							
I repeated my affirmation(s) and consciously reprogrammed my chatter brain's self-talk.							
I reflected on the Mindful Brain Fuel daily inspiration and quote of the day.							
I initiated my action step(s) for today.							
I exercised.							
In the Evening:							
I checked off the items I completed on the daily plan.							
I answered the self-reflection question.							
I jotted down my thoughts about my journey.							
I ended my day by smiling and saying, "I am grateful for this day and the positive shift I created in my life today!"							
Bonus Activities:							
I meditated.							
I completed a random act of kindness.							
I paid it forward.							
I read an inspirational book.							
I experienced AWE!							
Other: _____							

WEEK TWELVE

Spirituality

DAY 1

Belief

Do you believe there is a higher power in the universe? Do you consider yourself religious, spiritual, or both? Why have you adopted that belief? According to a 2023 Pew Research Center study on "Spirituality Among Americans," 7 in 10 U.S. adults describe themselves as spiritual in some way, including 22% who are spiritual but not religious. Although Americans have become less likely to identify with an organized religion, the survey shows that there is widespread belief in spirits or a spiritual realm beyond this world. The survey indicated that:

- 83% of all U.S. adults believe people have a soul or spirit in addition to their physical body.

- 81% say there is something spiritual beyond the natural world, even if we cannot see it.

- 74% say there are some things that science cannot possibly explain.

- 45% say they have had a sudden feeling of connection with something from beyond this world.

- 38% say they have had a strong feeling that someone who has passed away was communicating with them from beyond this world.

- 30% say they have personally encountered a spirit or unseen spiritual force.

Overall, 70% of US adults can be considered "spiritual" in some way, because they think of themselves as spiritual people or say spirituality is very important in their lives.

This week we'll explore some principles related to spirituality. I'll share some of my beliefs but want to make it clear that I'm not promoting any religion or spiritual community. Only you can decide what spiritual practice or religious doctrine nourishes your soul and fosters your connection to the world. I believe that those of us exploring personal development and enlightenment often engage in spiritual practices and activities such as prayer, meditation, or yoga to nurture our spiritual growth, while others prefer religious ceremonies and traditions that provide structure and meaning in their lives.

Spirituality is a deeply personal and individual experience, as well as a broad and multifaceted concept that involves a sense of connection to something greater than yourself. Having spiritual beliefs can lead to a deeper understanding of life's purpose and meaning, and encompass universal components that include a belief system, a sense of belonging, inner peace, personal growth, compassion and altruism, rituals and practices, community, and ethical living. I believe that by integrating these components into our lives, we cultivate a richer, more meaningful journey while on earth.

I'm the master of my shift!

AFFIRMATION

I am connected to my divine light and share it joyously with the world.

Week Twelve — Day 1

Unveiling Your True Self

What does spirituality mean to you?

_____
_____
_____
_____
_____
_____
_____
_____
_____
_____
_____
_____
_____
_____
_____
_____

We are not human beings having a spiritual experience;
we are spiritual beings having a human experience.
– Pierre Teilhard de Chardin

WEEK TWELVE

Spirituality

DAY 2

Faith

Various religious and philosophical traditions interpret and describe faith in different ways such as:

- A deep confidence or reliance on something or someone beyond yourself.

- The optimistic expectation or anticipation of positive outcomes.

- A willingness to let go of control and submit to a higher power or divine plan.

- Holding beliefs that provide a sense of purpose and understanding of the universe and your place in it.

I believe that faith also embodies having the courage to uphold, challenge, and evolve your beliefs. An example of this is the inspirational story of Malala Yousafzai, the Pakistani girl who became an advocate for girls' education. In 2012, she was shot in the head by the Taliban for speaking out. Malala survived the attack and continued her advocacy, becoming the youngest-ever Nobel Prize laureate. Despite ongoing threats, she has expanded her advocacy to include girls affected by the COVID-19 pandemic, climate change, and other global crises. Her unwavering faith in the power of education to transform lives and her courage to speak out in the face of adversity continues to inspire people around the world.

We also see faith demonstrated every day by the Ukrainian people. Since the Russian invasion of Ukraine in 2022, countless stories have emerged of ordinary Ukrainians showing extraordinary faith, hope, and courage. From soldiers defending their homeland to civilians providing aid, the Ukrainian people have demonstrated resilience and bravery in the face of overwhelming odds. Churches and faith-based organizations have played a significant role, offering spiritual support and humanitarian aid to those affected by the conflict. Their unwavering determination to protect their country and preserve their way of life is faith and courage in action.

In 2020, the deaths of two African Americans, George Floyd and Breonna Taylor, at the hands of police sparked worldwide protests. Despite the pain of losing their loved ones, their families have shown immense courage and faith in their pursuit of justice by turning their grief into a powerful force for change, advocating for police reform and racial justice. Their faith in the possibility of a better, more just society and their unwavering hope for a future free from racial discrimination has inspired millions to join the fight for equality.

I'm the master of my shift!

AFFIRMATION

My faith guides me toward my highest good.

Week Twelve

Day 2

Unveiling Your True Self

How is your faith evolving as you gain more wisdom?

_____
_____
_____
_____
_____
_____
_____
_____
_____
_____
_____
_____
_____
_____

Faith is taking the first step even when you don't see the whole staircase.
– Martin Luther King Jr.

Week Twelve

Spirituality

Day 3

Trust

In Week Ten, Day 2, I discussed being a trustworthy person. Today, I'll broaden that perspective to explore the idea that trust is born from faith and we practice faith and trust both unconsciously and consciously.

We unconsciously put our faith and trust in people we don't know every day. We have faith that other people have the expertise and integrity to do their best in their chosen occupations. Think of all the things you encounter every day that you unconsciously take for granted. For instance, when you

- step into an elevator you expect to arrive at your chosen floor safely;
- drive your car or travel by bus, train, or plane, you trust that the mechanic has maintained the equipment properly;
- go into a store, apartment building, or skyscraper, you trust that the building was constructed to code using quality materials so it won't collapse;
- flip a light switch, you expect light;
- turn on a faucet, you expect clean, hot and cold water;
- go to your favorite restaurant, you expect fresh food prepared in a clean kitchen so you don't get food poisoning, and the list goes on.

On the other hand, we consciously place faith and trust in others as shown through the story of Leon Logothetis who relied solely on the kindness of strangers to sustain his global adventure. In his book *The Kindness Diaries*, he tells the story of setting out on his journey with no money, trusting that people would help him with food, shelter, and support. Throughout his journey, he met many people who opened their homes and hearts to him, reaffirming his faith in humanity. This journey not only demonstrated his trust in others but also how those he met reciprocated their faith and trust in him by inviting him into their homes and sharing their resources.

These examples show that we have faith and trust in our fellow human beings, which is great news and quite reassuring. However, in addition to placing our trust in others, many of us also consciously put faith in a higher power through prayer. Prayer takes faith into our hearts and souls, where we take a step into the unknown—the place of believing that there is a universal energy, power, or divine presence that we can't see but we trust it exists—that's spirituality.

I'm the master of my shift!

AFFIRMATION

My faith gives me strength and courage.

Week Twelve — Day 3

Unveiling Your True Self

How has your faith evolved into trust in your life?

_____
_____
_____
_____
_____
_____
_____
_____
_____
_____
_____
_____
_____
_____
_____

None of us knows what might happen even the next minute, yet still we go forward. Because we trust. Because we have Faith.
– Paulo Coelho

Week Twelve

Spirituality

Day 4

Hope

Hope is an optimistic state of mind. It represents envisioning positive outcomes and having the confidence and motivation to achieve your vision even in the face of adversity or uncertainty. Hope is a fundamental human emotion that plays a critical role in our well-being and resilience, and it stems from our spiritual or religious faith, personal beliefs, relationships with others, and past experiences with overcoming challenges.

When you have hope, you usually believe that you have some control over the outcome. Hope differs from wishing by being more grounded in reality. Hope involves acknowledging challenges but also believing that there is a possibility to overcome them. For example, "I hope to recover from this illness." To achieve this vision, action steps might include taking medication, following medical advice, or making lifestyle changes.

Wishing, on the other hand, is passive and more about a desire. It usually comes without the expectation or effort to make it come true. When you make a wish, you may not believe it could happen so you don't make a plan to make it happen—the wish remains a dream. Wishing implies that we have less personal control and the wish may be unrealistic or less grounded in what is possible. Wishes focus more on an ideal scenario or fantasy. For example, "I wish I could fly." This statement expresses a desire for something that isn't possible in reality, and there is no action or belief behind it that makes it likely to happen.

Inspiring stories of hope range from individual achievements to solving global issues. For example:

- Richard Jenkins, a young man from Philadelphia, was homeless as a child, spending nights in shelters and motels. Despite his challenges, he excelled at school and was determined to break the cycle of poverty. His hard work paid off when he was accepted into Harvard University on a full scholarship.

- A group of engineers and environmentalists in Kenya developed a sustainable solution to reduce plastic pollution by turning plastic waste into bricks. These bricks are more durable than concrete and provide an affordable alternative building material. The initiative, started by Nzambi Matee, addresses both environmental and housing issues, offering hope for cleaner cities and more affordable housing solutions.

I'm the master of my shift!

AFFIRMATION

I am open to the miracles of life.

WEEK TWELVE — — — — — — — — — — — **DAY 4**

Unveiling Your True Self

What do you hope for and why?

_____
_____
_____
_____
_____
_____
_____
_____
_____
_____
_____
_____
_____
_____
_____

The pessimist complains about the wind; the optimist expects it to change; the realist adjusts the sails.
– William Arthur Ward

WEEK TWELVE

Spirituality

DAY 5

Vulnerability

Humans are vulnerable beings. The *Oxford Dictionary* defines vulnerability as the quality or state of being exposed to the possibility of being attacked or harmed, either physically or emotionally. In broad terms that means we are all vulnerable everywhere, at all times, which in today's society is a sad fact that can lead to living in fear. Although it's important to be realistic and acknowledge that we're vulnerable, it's also important to go beyond the fear associated with vulnerability and engage spiritually with faith, hope, and trust as noted in the stories I've shared the past few days.

Since the purpose of this program is to help you raise your consciousness and live life optimistically, let's leave the negative in the rear-view and look at the positive aspects of vulnerability. To illustrate this, let's look at the story of Paul Kalanithi, a neurosurgeon and author of the memoir *When Breath Becomes Air*. In his book, Paul describes the profound trust that exists between doctors and patients. After being diagnosed with terminal cancer, he found himself on both sides of this trust relationship. As a doctor, he had been trusted with his patients' lives; as a patient, he became vulnerable and had to place his faith in his own doctors, showing that vulnerability is truly a two-way street.

We also demonstrate vulnerability when we share information with others. However, in doing so we must be cognizant to share the right information with the right person at the right time. We certainly shouldn't share personal details with every person we meet, and we need to distinguish between what we share personally versus what's appropriate to share professionally. It's important to trust our instincts—our gut brain—and take time to reflect on our feelings and needs before sharing personal information and only share with someone we trust—someone who's shown they can be supportive and understanding.

Being vulnerable relates to our authenticity and allows us to be our true selves, rather than projecting a façade of how we want others to perceive us. When we open our hearts and are genuine and honest with others, we circulate faith and trust, which encourages others to be open and vulnerable with us. Although this isn't always easy, it's a powerful tool for personal growth and can help build closer personal relationships and professional connections.

I'm the master of my shift!

AFFIRMATION

I an genuine, open, and honest.

WEEK TWELVE

DAY 5

Unveiling Your True Self

What does spiritual vulnerability mean to you? What helps you be open and vulnerable with others?

_____
_____
_____
_____
_____
_____
_____
_____
_____
_____
_____
_____
_____
_____
_____

We cultivate love when we allow our most vulnerable and powerful selves to be deeply seen and known, and when we honor the spiritual connection that grows from that offering with trust, respect, kindness, and affection.
– **Brene Brown**

Week Twelve

Spirituality

Day 6

Intuition

Intuition—that feeling in your gut—you know the one when you get butterflies that give you a sudden insight, feeling about making an important decision, or a sense of peace when you've settled on a particular course of action. This feeling is different from using analytical reasoning, which relies on conscious thought processes and logical deductions. Intuition, or perhaps better described as *spiritual intuition* emerges from deep within our soul and subconscious mind. It's often described as a "gut feeling" or an inner knowing that transcends rational explanation.

Embrace your power of spiritual intuition! It isn't bound by the constraints of time and space and draws from a universal source of wisdom that is always available to those who are open to receiving it. Your inner voice or gut brain will guide you toward being your true self. It will uphold your core values, truth, and authenticity by transcending the boundaries of rational thought and tapping into your soul—your source of wisdom.

There is a relatively new field of scientific study that blends neuroscience, psychology, and the concept of the "gut feeling" to understand how our gut brain relates to the brain in our heads. Studies have shown that gut feelings can be remarkably accurate in certain scenarios, such as making snap judgments about people or assessing risky situations. This accuracy may stem from the brain's ability to process complex information rapidly, using the gut as a source of somatic markers or bodily responses that guide decisions.

Intuition can manifest as a quick, automatic response to a situation or a feeling that you're supposed to take a particular road in life. An example of making a quick decision in a high-pressure situation is Captain Sully Sullenberger's emergency landing on the Hudson River. On January 15, 2009, he was piloting US Airways Flight 1549 when the plane struck a flock of geese, causing both engines to fail. In the critical moments that followed, Sully's intuition told him that trying to return to the airport was too risky. Trusting his gut instinct and years of experience, he successfully landed the plane on the river, saving all 155 passengers and crew members on board.

An example of following your intuition for a long-term life decision is Jim Carrey's vision to write himself a check for $10 million for acting services rendered, dated a couple of years in the future. Jim kept the check in his wallet, trusting his intuition that he would eventually be able to cash it, which he did when he received a $10 million payment for his role in *Dumb and Dumber*. This story illustrates how trusting your intuition, combined with visualization and perseverance, can help turn dreams into reality.

I'm the master of my shift!

AFFIRMATION

I am tuned into my spiritual intuition.

WEEK TWELVE — — — — — — — — — — **DAY 6**

Unveiling Your True Self

Do you follow your intuition? Why or why not?

_____
_____
_____
_____
_____
_____
_____
_____
_____
_____
_____
_____
_____
_____
_____

Intuition is a very powerful thing, more powerful than intellect, in my opinion.
– Steve Jobs

WEEK TWELVE

Spirituality

DAY 7

Spirit

Spirit is the nonphysical part of us that is our essence—our soul—that place where infinite love, innate joy, wisdom, and character live. A strong spirit catapults us far beyond surviving life's challenges to thriving with grace, peace, and love. Our spirit is the part of us that can carry us through anything but may be one of the most neglected aspects of our personal development. Just as we exercise to condition our bodies, a healthy spirit needs to be nurtured through a purposeful practice like you're cultivating through this fifteen-week journey.

Developing your spiritual essence is about nurturing the core of who you are beyond the superficialities of the world. Living from your spiritual essence is to live in harmony with your authentic self. Finding your essence is a lifelong pursuit of self-discovery that gradually reveals the timeless, boundless part of who you are. Through self-awareness, stillness, letting go of ego, and embracing compassion, you can awaken the spiritual power that resides within you.

As you grow spiritually, you will find that external achievements, while still valuable, pale in comparison to the inner peace, joy, and fulfillment that come from living a life rooted in your essence. When you align with your spiritual core, you live not just for yourself but for something greater—a purpose that transcends the material world and connects you to the infinite love and wisdom of the universe.

One of the most powerful true stories about developing spiritual essence comes from the life of Nelson Mandela, the former president of South Africa and anti-apartheid revolutionary who was in prison for 27 years for speaking against apartheid. His journey of spiritual growth and inner transformation is an inspiring testament to the power of faith, forgiveness, and perseverance in the face of unimaginable challenges and shows that sometimes, it's in the darkest, most challenging moments that your spirit is tested and strengthened. By choosing forgiveness over vengeance, love over hate, and unity over division, Mandela became a symbol of hope and resilience for the world and his journey continues to inspire people to seek inner peace, forgiveness, and compassion, even in the face of adversity.

Let your life's journey be one of courage, trust, and faith, knowing that your personal exploration brings you closer to the truest, most profound version of yourself.

I'm the master of my shift!

AFFIRMATION

I radiate love and joy.

WEEK TWELVE — — — — — — — — — — **DAY 7**

Unveiling Your True Self

What does spiritual essence mean to you and why?

_____
_____
_____
_____
_____
_____
_____
_____
_____
_____
_____
_____
_____
_____
_____

**Knowing others is intelligence; knowing yourself is true wisdom.
Mastering others is strength; mastering yourself is true power.
– Lao Tzu**

WEEK 13

CONNECTEDNESS

The Shift Code Daily Routine Checklist

WEEK THIRTEEN	*Connectedness*	Day 1	Day 2	Day 3	Day 4	Day 5	Day 6	Day 7
In the Morning:									
I began my day by smiling and saying, "I am grateful for this day and the positive shift I'm creating in my life!"							
I read the daily action plan in my workbook.							
I made note of the focus of my affirmation(s) and self-talk for the day.							
I identified one or more action steps for the day.							
During the Day:								
I repeated my affirmation(s) and consciously reprogrammed my chatter brain's self-talk.							
I reflected on the Mindful Brain Fuel daily inspiration and quote of the day.							
I initiated my action step(s) for today.							
I exercised.							
In the Evening:								
I checked off the items I completed on the daily plan.							
I answered the self-reflection question.							
I jotted down my thoughts about my journey.							
I ended my day by smiling and saying, "I am grateful for this day and the positive shift I created in my life today!"							
Bonus Activities:								
I meditated.							
I completed a random act of kindness.							
I paid it forward.							
I read an inspirational book.							
I experienced AWE!							
Other: _____							

Week Thirteen

Connectedness

Day 1

Love

In today's fast-paced world, it's easy to feel disconnected from ourselves and those around us. We become so wrapped up in juggling schedules and moving from one activity to another that we neglect our spiritual connections to ourselves, our family, and our friends. I believe becoming spiritually connected and being a loving person is more important than ever. No matter what your belief system is, taking time to connect with your spiritual essence every day through the daily routine in this journey, will help you remain grounded in values like compassion, kindness, and empathy. These aren't just nice-to-have qualities—they form the core of living a connected, enriched, and loving life.

An example of love and spiritual connection can be seen in the work of Jonny Benjamin, a man who was saved by a stranger on a bridge. Jonny was struggling with mental health issues and had reached a point of despair, planning to end his life by jumping off a bridge in London. As he stood on the edge, a stranger named Neil Laybourn walked by, and instead of ignoring Jonny, Neil stopped to talk with him. Neil didn't know Jonny, but his heart opened to him in that moment. He gently spoke words of encouragement and hope, convincing Jonny to step away from the edge and choose life.

Years later, Jonny, who became an advocate for mental health, launched a campaign to find the man who saved him so he could thank him properly. They were reunited, and Jonny credits Neil's act of kindness with completely changing the course of his life. Jonny's story inspired many others to reach out, share their struggles, and offer support.

This story shows how one moment of loving outreach from one human being to another can be life-altering. Neil's simple act of kindness in that critical moment transformed Jonny's life, and Jonny went on to help others in return, creating a chain of compassion and love.

When we nurture that spiritual connection, we start seeing the good in ourselves and others. We're more likely to act from a place of love, knowing that even the smallest act of kindness can make a world of difference. It's a reminder that we're all part of something bigger—and love, when shared freely, has the power to change lives.

I'm the master of my shift!

AFFIRMATION

The love in my heart sparks a chain reaction of positive connections throughout my life.

WEEK THIRTEEN — — — — — — — — — — **DAY 1**

Unveiling Your True Self

When have you used the power of love to transform difficult situations?

We rise by lifting others.
– Robert Ingersoll

Week Thirteen

Connectedness

Day 2

Belonging

Belonging is a deep spiritual need that we all share, and it's a powerful force in shaping our sense of self and our connection to the world. Whether we find it through family, friends, coworkers, or social groups, that sense of belonging helps us feel rooted, valued, and connected to something larger than ourselves. However, having a sense of belonging is much more than simply being part of a group; it's about feeling seen, heard, and accepted for who we truly are and it requires nurturing on our part.

Cultivating our sense of belonging and connectedness requires intentionality, both in how we interact with others and how we care for our own emotional and spiritual well-being. A few ways to develop your sense of belonging include:

- Be present and engaged. Have the courtesy to show genuine interest in what others have to say by putting down your phone, making eye contact, and listening attentively.
- Don't judge. Accept people as they are. Offering empathy, understanding, or reassurance can validate someone's thoughts, feelings, or contributions.
- Be authentic. When appropriate, share your own challenges, be open about your experiences, and create a space for others to do the same. This builds trust, which is essential for creating a sense of belonging. This builds trust, which is essential for creating a sense of belonging.
- Be inclusive. Reach out to folks outside your immediate circle. Inviting new people into conversations, decision-making, and activities will expand your sense of belonging as well as those with whom you engage.
- Connect to your spiritual essence. Taking time to meditate, pray, or simply be quiet in nature can help you feel connected to the larger whole. Your feeling of connectedness to the infinite energy (the unseen spirit) of the universe will help you tap into the love, compassion, and understanding you were born to share throughout your life.

These simple actions are gifts that benefit not only those around you but also your own heart and soul. They can create environments where both you and others feel a deep sense of belonging and connectedness, and when we feel like we belong, we're more likely to act with love, kindness, and empathy, which in turn creates a ripple of positivity in the world around us.

I'm the master of my shift!

AFFIRMATION

I expand my sense of belonging by including and welcoming new people into my life and conversations.

WEEK THIRTEEN — **DAY 2**

Unveiling Your True Self

What negative thoughts or beliefs might be holding you back from feeling like you belong in certain spaces, and how can you reframe them.

_____
_____
_____
_____
_____
_____
_____
_____
_____
_____
_____
_____
_____
_____
_____

The best way to find yourself is to lose yourself in the service of others.
– Mahatma Gandhi

Week Thirteen

Connectedness

Day 3

Purpose

Having a sense of purpose that aligns with your core values and spiritual essence is a key factor in living a fulfilled and connected life. Purpose in this sense is much bigger than setting goals and checking tasks off your daily to-do list. It's about aligning your values with your personal mission to define how you want to live and be remembered. For instance, would you like to be described as the best mom, dad, or friend ever? Or, how about a loving, compassionate, or kind person, an optimist, or an inspirational leader with the utmost integrity?

Only through deep introspection will you be able to find your purpose. You'll know it when it comes to you because it will resonate deeply with who you are at your core and align with your overarching mission in life. When your purpose is in harmony with your inner beliefs, it will drive you forward and connect you to the world in a profound way. Your purpose will give you a reason to get up in the morning, enhance your physical and mental well-being, and even contribute to you feeling more energetic, robust, and happier. This is because purpose gives you a reason to keep moving forward, even when the road is difficult.

However, true purpose is more than just an intellectual pursuit. It grows from a deep connection to our values and a desire to contribute to the greater good. When your purpose aligns with your spiritual essence—your deepest sense of self—it becomes a guiding force that keeps you grounded and focused. In other words, this alignment ensures that your actions fulfill your personal goals in a way that reflects your core values and personal mission statement.

A sense of purpose also enhances our connection to others. Purpose is inherently social and contributes to our interactions and relationships. When our overarching purpose is in alignment with our life's mission, we often find ourselves surrounded by a community of like-minded individuals who share our values and vision. This connection to others strengthens our sense of belonging, making us feel that we are part of something larger than ourselves.

Ultimately, living with purpose in alignment with your core values and mission can transform your life by giving you clarity, direction, and a deeper connection to the world. By living authentically and purposefully, you can create a life that not only brings fulfillment but also uplifts those around you.

I'm the master of my shift!

AFFIRMATION

My purpose fills me with energy and motivates me to strengthen my connections with others.

WEEK THIRTEEN — — — — — — — — — — **DAY 3**

Unveiling Your True Self

What is your life's overarching purpose? How does it align with your personal mission?

_____
_____
_____
_____
_____
_____
_____
_____
_____
_____
_____
_____
_____
_____
_____
_____

**The meaning of life is to find your gift. The purpose of life is to give it away.
– Pablo Picasso**

Week Thirteen

Connectedness

Day 4

Grace

We often hear about the power of living with gratitude, but grace, its often-overlooked partner, carries its own profound benefits. Grace is about more than just elegance or forgiveness—it's about moving through life with a sense of harmony, presence, and divine love. When we embrace grace, we open ourselves to courage, patience, and the humor needed to face life's challenges. It's a deep, instinctual knowing that we are connected to something greater than ourselves.

My mother lived to the age of 101. She persevered through many life altering challenges including the passing of her mother and father by age 7, living through the Great Depression on her grandparents' farm in Missouri, and the death of a daughter at age 2. She often spoke of living from the essence of her soul and focusing on living life with grace as described by Maya Angelou: "A woman in harmony with her spirit is like a river flowing. She goes where she will without pretense and arrives at her destination prepared to be herself and only herself."

As epitomized by my mom, grace has the ability to transform lives and situations. It encourages us to respond with kindness, love, and acceptance rather than react to difficulties with anger or frustration. Grace is available to everyone, at any moment, and it doesn't cost a thing. It's not tied to any specific religion but rather serves as a universal force that uplifts and heals.

Acts of grace are contagious and can spread from one person to another, creating waves of kindness and hope. Something as simple as a warm hug, a hot meal, or a word of encouragement can be a profound expression of grace, bringing light to someone in need. During times of war, famine, or personal struggle, grace has the power to sustain people, giving them the strength to endure and the compassion to care for others.

Grace reminds us that even after someone passes away, their legacy can live on through the grace they showed in their lives. Princess Diana, for example, demonstrated grace by reaching out to those suffering from AIDS and advocating for landmine survivors. Her actions changed the world, proving that grace can make a lasting impact.

In a world that often feels chaotic and challenging, grace offers a way to live with peace, clarity, and humility. It allows us to flow through life with trust and faith, helping us heal old wounds and see new perspectives. Grace is a powerful, life-changing force that connects us to ourselves, others, and the world around us.

I'm the master of my shift!

AFFIRMATION

Grace flows through me, allowing me to face challenges with patience, courage, and humor.

WEEK THIRTEEN

Unveiling Your True Self

DAY 4

How do you display grace in your life?

___

Grace is not part of consciousness; it is the amount of light in our souls, not knowledge nor reason.
– Pope Francis

Week Thirteen — Day 5

Connectedness — *Joy*

I love the word joy—possibly because my name is Gay and people often call me Joy. Plus, it always brings a smile to my face. Joy, much like purpose and gratitude, is a powerful force that brings us a sense of well-being, fulfillment, and connection to the world around us. It goes beyond fleeting happiness or a brief moment of pleasure. Joy is a deeper, more enduring state of being that arises when we are aligned with our core values and connected to what matters most in life.

True joy is often experienced when we feel a sense of purpose or when we've made progress toward something meaningful. It's the feeling of achieving something important, not just for ourselves but often in the context of others. As noted in Positive Psychology, joy can be found in both the anticipation of achieving a goal and in the fulfillment of that goal. Joy is about more than just personal success. It's about living in harmony with your values and engaging in activities that make a difference in your life and in the lives of others.

There's also a social element to joy. Studies show that joy is often shared, and it thrives in relationships and communities. Whether it's the laughter shared among friends, the celebration of a loved one's achievements, or the collective energy in a moment of shared success, joy connects us. It brings us closer to others and helps us build stronger, more meaningful relationships.

Spiritually, joy can be seen as an alignment with the greater good. It is often linked to feelings of transcendence—when we rise above the ordinary and feel connected to something much larger than ourselves. This sense of connectedness helps us view life from a broader perspective, bringing clarity and peace even during challenging times.

In essence, joy is both an individual and collective experience. It's cultivated through gratitude, purpose, and meaningful connections, and when we nurture it, joy brings us closer to ourselves, to others, and to the world. It teaches us that life is about more than just getting through the day. It's about truly living with intention, presence, and love.

I'm the master of my shift!

AFFIRMATION

I radiate and spread joy throughout my life.

WEEK THIRTEEN   **DAY 5**

Unveiling Your True Self

How do you cultivate joy in your life?

_____
_____
_____
_____
_____
_____
_____
_____
_____
_____
_____
_____
_____
_____
_____

Scatter joy.
– Ralph Waldo Emerson

Week Thirteen — Day 6

Connectedness — *Peace*

Living a peaceful life is a journey of inner harmony, balance, and intentionality. True peace, as described in many philosophies like Taoism and reflected in peaceful societies around the world, begins within us. It's not merely the absence of conflict but the presence of tranquility, clarity, and a deep connection with the flow of life.

One key to cultivating a peaceful life is understanding that peace is both an internal and external practice. Internally, peace is about self-awareness and letting go of attachments and desires that disturb our inner equilibrium. The Tao Te Ching teaches that we should flow naturally with life, embracing the present moment without forcing outcomes or resisting the natural rhythm of things. This concept of "Wu wei" or "non-action," reminds us that often the best action is to align ourselves with the natural order, allowing life to unfold without unnecessary interference.

Externally, peace is fostered through our interactions with others and the world. Peaceful societies, whether in parts of the world where conflict is minimal or in personal relationships, are built on reciprocity, kindness, and understanding.

Positive interactions between people create a web of connectedness that sustains harmony. By showing respect, being mindful in communication, and leading with empathy, we contribute to a more peaceful environment, both in our homes and communities.

Living peacefully also means accepting the interconnectedness of all things. The Taoist idea of the "Yin and Yang" teaches that life is about balance—light and dark, activity and rest, joy and sorrow. A peaceful life acknowledges this balance and seeks harmony in all aspects of existence, embracing both the ups and downs as necessary parts of a unified whole.

Ultimately, peace is something we cultivate daily, through our thoughts, actions, and relationships. By living in alignment with our core values, being present in the moment, and fostering positive interactions with others, we can create a peaceful life for ourselves and contribute to a more harmonious world. Peace is not just an ideal; it is a way of living, a practice that begins within and radiates outward.

I'm the master of my shift!

AFFIRMATION

I embrace peace in my heart and allow it to guide my thoughts and actions.

WEEK THIRTEEN — — — — — — — — — — **DAY 6**

Unveiling Your True Self

What does living peacefully mean to you and how are you demonstrating it in your life?

_____
_____
_____
_____
_____
_____
_____
_____
_____
_____
_____
_____
_____
_____
_____

Those who are at peace within themselves are also at peace with the world.
– Lao Tzu

WEEK THIRTEEN

Connectedness

DAY 7

Unity

In *The Science of Mind*, Ernest Holmes teaches that we are all connected through a universal intelligence, a divine energy that permeates everything. This energy, often referred to as Spirit or the Infinite, is the essence of life itself. Holmes believed that we are all expressions of this same source—meaning that at our core, we are deeply interconnected. This understanding brings a profound realization: what affects one of us, in some way, affects all of us.

Holmes explains that our thoughts, beliefs, and actions have a ripple effect in the world. When we think positively, embrace love, and act with kindness, we contribute to the greater good, sending out waves of positive energy that touch others. Conversely, when we harbor negativity or act out of fear or anger, we can contribute to disconnection and discord. Our inner world is linked to the outer world, and our personal energy influences the collective energy of humanity.

This sense of connection is not just spiritual—it is also practical. We see it in how communities function, how relationships grow, and how acts of kindness can uplift not just the recipient but the giver and even the observer. Holmes reminds us that "thoughts are things," and by focusing on thoughts that unite and heal, we actively contribute to creating a more connected, harmonious world.

Moreover, recognizing our interconnectedness can shift how we approach life's challenges. It helps us see that we are not alone in our struggles, as others are walking similar paths. When we understand that we are all part of the same spiritual fabric, it becomes easier to offer compassion, empathy, and support to those around us. We start to understand that separation is an illusion, and our individual well-being is tied to the well-being of others.

Living with this awareness brings a sense of peace and responsibility. By acknowledging our oneness with others and the world, we step into a role of co-creating a better reality. As Holmes wrote, "We are all inlets to the same ocean, and through this understanding, we find the path to true peace, love, and unity." It's a powerful reminder that we are, indeed, all connected and our choices shape not only our lives but the collective experience of humanity.

I'm the master of my shift!

AFFIRMATION

I choose to act from a place of love, knowing that what I do for others, I do for myself.

WEEK THIRTEEN   **DAY 7**

Unveiling Your True Self

How do your thoughts and actions contribute to the sense of oneness and connection with others?

Life is a mirror and will reflect back to the thinker what he thinks into it.
– Ernest Holmes

WEEK 14

LIFE

The Shift Code Daily Routine Checklist

**WEEK FOURTEEN	*Life***	Day 1	Day 2	Day 3	Day 4	Day 5	Day 6	Day 7
In the Morning:							
I began my day by smiling and saying, "I am grateful for this day and the positive shift I'm creating in my life!"							
I read the daily action plan in my workbook.							
I made note of the focus of my affirmation(s) and self-talk for the day.							
I identified one or more action steps for the day.							
During the Day:							
I repeated my affirmation(s) and consciously reprogrammed my chatter brain's self-talk.							
I reflected on the Mindful Brain Fuel daily inspiration and quote of the day.							
I initiated my action step(s) for today.							
I exercised.							
In the Evening:							
I checked off the items I completed on the daily plan.							
I answered the self-reflection question.							
I jotted down my thoughts about my journey.							
I ended my day by smiling and saying, "I am grateful for this day and the positive shift I created in my life today!"							
Bonus Activities:							
I meditated.							
I completed a random act of kindness.							
I paid it forward.							
I read an inspirational book.							
I experienced AWE!							
Other: _____							

WEEK FOURTEEN

Life

DAY 1

Awe

Some words are just plain cool, and "awe" is one of them. Think about how we stretch it out and sing it when we're happy, "aaaaaaaaaaa," or exclaim, "awesome!" when something excites us. Experiencing awe ignites dramatic feelings in our core and let's our soul sing.

Awe is one of those emotions that lights up something deep within us. It's a feeling we can't quite put into words, yet it resonates so strongly that it has the power to stop us in our tracks. Whether it's standing on a mountaintop, watching a glorious sunset, or gazing up at the stars, awe connects us to something much larger than ourselves. It's more than just an "awesome" moment; it's an invitation to step outside of our day-to-day worries and enjoy life from a more inspirational viewpoint.

One of the most transformative aspects of awe is its ability to shift our focus from ourselves to the collective whole. When we experience awe, we feel small, but at the same time, free and uninhibited. Our ego departs stage left, which leaves us more open, creative, joyful, and blessed with a deep sense of gratitude for the world around us. In these moments, awe merges with spirituality and our soul's speak the pure language of love, compassion, and unity.

Interestingly, awe doesn't always require monumental experiences. It's something you can find in everyday moments—clouds floating like angel wings or cute puppy dogs, a beautiful piece of music, or hummingbirds drinking the sweet nectar of a flower. Awe is especially important during challenging times by helping us shift our perspective and turn our focus from negativity to seeing life's beauty and possibilities.

At its core, awe reminds us that we're part of a much larger narrative. It grounds us in a sense of connectedness, encourages gratitude, and helps us live more mindfully. When we experience awe, we're reminded that life isn't just about what's right in front of us. It's about tapping into something more expansive, something that enriches our spirit and deepens our connection to the world.

I'm the master of my shift!

AFFIRMATION

I embrace the wonder in everyday moments and find joy in the simple things.

WEEK FOURTEEN — **DAY 1**

Unveiling Your True Self

What simple, daily occurrences could you appreciate more to evoke a sense of awe?

_____
_____
_____
_____
_____
_____
_____
_____
_____
_____
_____
_____
_____
_____
_____
_____

Wonder is the beginning of wisdom.
– Socrates

Week Fourteen

Life

Day 2

Curiosity

Curiosity is a powerful force that can enrich our lives in unexpected ways. When we nurture our sense of curiosity, we open ourselves to new experiences, perspectives, and opportunities for growth. One of the greatest benefits of curiosity is its ability to keep our minds active and engaged. Studies suggest that curious people tend to live longer, healthier lives, as they are more likely to challenge themselves and seek out stimulating, novel experiences that keep their minds sharp as they age.

In *A Curious Mind* by Brian Grazer, the celebrated film producer credits curiosity as his secret weapon for creativity, innovation, and success. Grazer explains how asking questions and being genuinely interested in others opened doors to opportunities and ideas that shaped his career. For him, curiosity isn't just about gathering knowledge; it's about forming meaningful connections with people. His "curiosity conversations," a practice of asking questions with no agenda other than learning, foster deeper understanding and new perspectives that fuel his creative endeavors.

In *MindFire* by Scott Berkun, curiosity is portrayed as a driving force behind innovation and creative breakthroughs. Berkun emphasizes that curiosity is more than just asking questions. It's about challenging assumptions, embracing uncertainty, and being willing to explore the unknown. By nurturing a curious mindset, we can break free from rigid thinking patterns and find innovative solutions to problems. Berkun's key message is that curiosity leads to intellectual freedom and empowers us to think differently, which is essential in today's world.

The Power of Curiosity by Kathy Taberner highlights how curiosity strengthens relationships by fostering empathy and open communication. According to Taberner, when we approach others with curiosity, we listen more intently, ask better questions, and gain insights into their experiences. This deepens our understanding and connection with them. She states that curiosity also plays a crucial role in personal growth, as it encourages us to challenge our limiting beliefs and explore new perspectives, leading to greater self-awareness.

Curiosity is a vital skill that expands our horizons by encouraging us to step outside our comfort zones and explore unfamiliar topics, experiences, and ideas. When we allow curiosity to guide us, we're more likely to delve into areas we might have otherwise overlooked, sparking new interests and passions that enrich our lives. Whether it's picking up a new hobby, exploring unfamiliar cultures, or learning about new scientific developments, curiosity invites us to see the world with fresh eyes and keeps our sense of wonder alive.

I'm the master of my shift!

AFFIRMATION

I embrace curiosity as a powerful force for growth and discovery in my life.

WEEK FOURTEEN — — — — — — — — — — **DAY 2**

Unveiling Your True Self

How do you handle uncertainty or unfamiliar topics? Are you more likely to avoid them, or approach them with curiosity?

_____
_____
_____
_____
_____
_____
_____
_____
_____
_____
_____
_____
_____
_____

Curiosity will conquer fear even more than bravery will.
– James Stephens

Week Fourteen

Life

Day 3

Humor

Laughter is basically a free workout for your mind, body, and soul, and who doesn't love free stuff? Honestly, if laughter were a pill, people would be shoving it into pill organizers like it's a daily vitamin. We all know that laughing feels good, but let's break down why it's truly one of life's best medicines. Spoiler alert: you won't even need a prescription.

First off, laughter is a stressbuster. It's like a magic spell that makes your worries vanish for a few glorious seconds. That annoying email from your boss? Poof! The mountain of laundry that may or may not collapse and trap you inside your home? Gone! Well, at least temporarily. When you laugh, your brain gets a hit of endorphins, and suddenly the world doesn't look quite so grim. It's like hitting the reset button on a bad day.

But the real kicker? Laughing is contagious. No, not like that sneeze on the subway you're desperately avoiding. I'm talking about the good kind of contagious. Ever notice how one person's laugh can set off a chain reaction? Next thing you know, everyone's giggling, even if they didn't catch the joke. And let's be honest, half the time the joke isn't even that funny. It's the absurdity of the laughter that gets you. And now, congratulations, you've turned a mundane moment into a memory.

Laughter is also a major social lubricant. Awkward first date? Cue a funny story about your dog chasing its tail until it falls over. You'll go from "Who's this stranger?" to "I could hang with this person" in no time. Studies even show that people are drawn to those with a good sense of humor, probably because life is just more fun with someone who can make you snort laugh.

And did you know laughter can burn calories? Okay, not as many as a treadmill, but it sure beats sweating it out in a gym. Ten to fifteen minutes of laughing can burn 10 to 40 calories. So really, that sitcom binge is "technically" cardio. You're welcome.

At the end of the day, laughter does more than just entertain. It's a full-body, mood-boosting, stress-reducing workout. So, go ahead, crack that joke. Your body and mind will thank you, and who knows, you might just give someone else the best medicine they didn't know they needed.

I'm the master of my shift!

AFFIRMATION

My laugh is contagious!

WEEK FOURTEEN — — — — — — — — — — **DAY 3**

Unveiling Your True Self

What makes you laugh?

_____
_____
_____
_____
_____
_____
_____
_____
_____
_____
_____
_____
_____
_____
_____
_____
_____

Laughter is the shortest distance between two people.
—Victor Borge

Week Fourteen

Life

Day 4

Passion

People tell you to "follow your passion" as if it's a GPS that'll lead you to fame, fortune, and maybe even a personal chef who specializes in breakfast burritos. But what does passion really mean, and why does everyone talk about it like it's the secret sauce to a fulfilling life?

First off, passion isn't just about doing something you love. It's about doing something that lights a fire inside you, the kind of fire that makes you lose track of time. You know that moment when you're so into what you're doing that suddenly it's midnight, and you've skipped dinner—that's passion. It's that internal drive that makes you push forward when everyone else has decided to call it a day and binge-watch TV.

Passion isn't always easy. Sometimes it's messy. Think about artists, athletes, or entrepreneurs. They don't just wake up every day singing "I'm walking on sunshine." Passion takes work. It's not all rainbows and motivational quotes. It's late nights, early mornings, and more coffee than should be legally allowed. But the thing is, when you're passionate about something, all that effort doesn't feel like a burden—it feels like purpose.

And here's a little secret no one tells you: Passion doesn't have to be a grand, earth-shattering thing. It can be small. You don't need to move to Paris to write the next great novel or launch a startup from your garage. Passion can be something as simple as perfecting your grandma's pie recipe or mastering the art of growing houseplants that, for once, don't die after a week. It's about finding joy in the process, not just the end result.

At the end of the day, passion is the fuel that keeps life interesting. It's what makes you feel alive, gives you something to strive for, and makes all the hard work worth it. So, go ahead and chase it, nurture it, and most importantly, let it guide you toward whatever makes your soul do a happy dance.

I'm the master of my shift!

AFFIRMATION

My passion fuels my success.

WEEK FOURTEEN

DAY 4

Unveiling Your True Self

What are you passionate about?

_____
_____
_____
_____
_____
_____
_____
_____
_____
_____
_____
_____
_____
_____
_____

Passion is the oxygen of the soul.
– Bill Butler

Week Fourteen

Life

Day 5

Endurance

Endurance is life's version of the ultimate marathon, except, instead of handing out medals at the end, you get wisdom, a few wrinkles, and maybe an extra helping of patience. Sticking with something over the long haul isn't exactly glamorous. Have you ever heard anyone say, "Wow, I endured so well today"? No, because endurance doesn't get the same applause as a quick win. Think about the people who've been branded as an "overnight success." It didn't really happen overnight. They've been trudging through the mud, uphill both ways, in the rain for years to make their dream come true. You know, doing the work, the fun stuff.

Endurance is about showing up, day after day, even when the excitement has fizzled out like the last sparkler on the Fourth of July. It's about plowing through the mundane, the tedious, and sometimes the downright frustrating. It's not the flashy, "look at me, I'm crushing it" part of success. No, endurance is more like, "Well, I didn't quit today, so that's a win."

Think about it, everything worth doing requires some level of endurance. As you're building your career, you'll need endurance for those moments when your boss emails you at 4:59 p.m. on a Friday asking for a 200-page report by Monday at 9:00 a.m. When you're training for a marathon, every mile brings a new level of exhaustion, but you keep going because at some point (hopefully, before mile 26), it's going to feel worth it. Starting a garden isn't all flowers and sunshine, you're going to battle weeds, bugs, and your neighbor's dog digging up your tomatoes. But if you endure, if you keep showing up, you'll eventually see the fruits (and veggies) of your labor.

Enduring isn't always easy and there are going to be moments when you feel like throwing in the towel. Heck, you might want to throw in the whole linen closet. But here's the thing—overcoming obstacles is what builds the real grit. It's not the easy wins that make you strong, it's the hard-fought battles that teach you resilience.

So, the next time life throws a few curveballs, just remember, you're in this for the long haul. And hey, you're enduring right now, you've made it to Week Fourteen of this 15-week journey! Keep going. The finish line is closer than you think!

I'm the master of my shift!

AFFIRMATION

Every day, I become more determined to achieve what I set out to do.

WEEK FOURTEEN — **DAY 5**

Unveiling Your True Self

What are you willing to endure to make your dreams come true?

Fall seven times, stand up eight.
– Japanese Proverb

Week Fourteen

Life

Day 6

Abundance

Abundance is one of those words that tends to get lumped in with yachts, private jets, and a closet full of shoes you'll never actually wear. True abundance is so much bigger than your bank account. Sure, financial freedom is great (who doesn't want to check their account balance without breaking into a cold sweat), but a truly abundant life goes far beyond what's in your wallet.

Abundance is all around us. Look outside. No, really—step outside for a second. Nature is the ultimate example of abundance. From the countless stars in the sky to the way flowers bloom year after year without asking for anything in return, the universe is constantly overflowing with beauty and growth. You don't need a million dollars to sit under a tree and appreciate the ridiculous number of leaves it produces every season or to take a deep breath of fresh air and feel grateful for the simple fact that you're alive to enjoy it.

But abundance doesn't stop at nature. It spills over into every aspect of life—our relationships, careers, and opportunities for personal growth. An abundant career isn't just about climbing the corporate ladder or adding extra zeros to your paycheck. It's about finding purpose, waking up excited (okay, maybe just semi-excited) about what you get to do each day. It's that sense of fulfillment that comes from knowing your work matters, that you're making an impact, no matter how small. That's real abundance.

And let's not forget relationships—love, connection, and community. Those are the true riches of life. Whether it's a deep conversation with a friend, a hug from someone you love, or even a laugh with a stranger, these moments fill us up in ways that no paycheck ever could. Life is abundant when we surround ourselves with people who lift us up and remind us that we're part of something bigger.

Bottom line: the universe offers abundance to everyone, and it's not limited to material wealth. It's about recognizing the blessings we already have and being open to receiving more—more love, more joy, more opportunities to grow. Life is abundant when we stop chasing and start appreciating.

I'm the master of my shift!

AFFIRMATION

The more I appreciate what I have, the more abundance I receive.

WEEK FOURTEEN — **DAY 6**

Unveiling Your True Self

What limiting beliefs might be holding you back from experiencing true abundance?

_____
_____
_____
_____
_____
_____
_____
_____
_____
_____
_____
_____
_____
_____
_____

Abundance is not something we acquire. It is something we tune into.
–Wayne Dyer

WEEK FOURTEEN

Life

DAY 7

Zest

Zest! It's not just the tangy kick in your lemonade or the key ingredient in a good marinara sauce. Zest is that extra oomph! that makes life more than just a series of snooze-worthy days on repeat. It's the spark, the enthusiasm, the full-bodied joy that gets you up in the morning with a smile (or at least without needing to hit the snooze button twelve times). Much like the necessity to experience awe every day, a day without zest is like a pizza without cheese or an ice cream sundae without chocolate sauce and the cherry on top!

So, what does it mean to live with zest? It's about embracing life with enthusiasm and seeing the world as a playground of possibilities. It's that extra pep in your step when you take on new challenges, whether it's learning how to salsa dance or finally tackling that dusty guitar in the corner of your living room. People with zest don't just exist—they thrive, turning even the mundane into a mini adventure.

Now, I'm not saying you need to jump out of bed every morning shouting "carpe diem!" while high-fiving the sunrise. But let's admit it, when was the last time you did something exciting that made you scream "awesome!" Zest is about finding joy in the small things: the sizzle of a hot skillet, the first sip of coffee, or that one song that makes you want to dance like no one's watching (even when everyone actually is). It's not about waiting for the perfect moment, it's about creating moments that make life worth savoring, like a perfectly zesty slice of key lime pie.

Zest doesn't just happen to you. You've got to bring it to the table. It's an attitude, a choice to show up for life with curiosity and a little bit of spunk. It's that feeling when you're so caught up in a great conversation that you forget to check your phone. Or when you try something new, fail gloriously, and laugh your way through it anyway.

At the end of the day, zest is about living life full-out, tasting all its flavors, even the spicy and unexpected ones. Because life, my friends, is way more fun when you live from A to Z—in Awe and with Zest!

I'm the master of my shift!

AFFIRMATION

I live every day with enthusiasm and a zest for life's adventures.

WEEK FOURTEEN — — — — — — — — — **DAY 7**

Unveiling Your True Self

What's one thing you can do today to bring more excitement into your routine?

_____
_____
_____
_____
_____
_____
_____
_____
_____
_____
_____
_____
_____
_____

Zest is the secret of all beauty. There is no beauty that is attractive without zest.
– Christian Dior

WEEK 15

Who Am I Now?

The Shift Code Daily Routine Checklist

WEEK FIFTEEN | *Who Am I Now?*	Day 1	Day 2	Day 3	Day 4	Day 5	Day 6	Day 7
In the Morning:							
I began my day by smiling and saying, "I am grateful for this day and the positive shift I'm creating in my life!"							
I read the daily action plan in my workbook.							
I made note of the focus of my affirmation(s) and self-talk for the day.							
I identified one or more action steps for the day.							
During the Day:							
I repeated my affirmation(s) and consciously reprogrammed my chatter brain's self-talk.							
I reflected on the Mindful Brain Fuel daily inspiration and quote of the day.							
I initiated my action step(s) for today.							
I exercised.							
In the Evening:							
I checked off the items I completed on the daily plan.							
I answered the self-reflection question.							
I jotted down my thoughts about my journey.							
I ended my day by smiling and saying, "I am grateful for this day and the positive shift I created in my life today!"							
Bonus Activities:							
I meditated.							
I completed a random act of kindness.							
I paid it forward.							
I read an inspirational book.							
I experienced AWE!							
Other: _____							

WEEK FIFTEEN

Who Am I Now?

DAY 1

My Dream!

Congratulations! You have persevered and made it to the final week of your journey to change your thoughts and change your life. This week will be spent reflecting on who you were when you started this program and who you are now.

Review your answer to the question on Week One, Day 1. "If you could do anything in life, knowing you would not fail, what would you do?"

- Would you have the same answer today as on Day 1?

- If not, why has your dream changed?

- Have your priorities shifted as a result of you evolving through this program?

- Do you have a new passion? What is it and how will you pursue it?

- Has your vision for your life grown or shifted based on your experiences in the program?

- How are your skills evolving in pursuit of your dream?

- Have you taken specific actions toward achieving your dream during the program? If not, why? If yes, what are the actions and their results?

- Moving forward, what are the first three steps you need to take to bring your dream closer to reality?

I'm the master of my shift!

AFFIRMATION

I am capable of achieving anything I set my mind to.

Week Fifteen

Day 1

Unveiling Your True Self

Revise or affirm your answer to, "If you could do anything in life, knowing you would not fail, what would you do?"

_____
_____
_____
_____
_____
_____
_____
_____
_____
_____
_____
_____
_____
_____

Don't look for your dreams to come true; look to become true to your dreams.
– Michael Bernard Beckwith

WEEK FIFTEEN

Who Am I Now?

DAY 2

My Interests and Talents

Review the list of your interests and talents you wrote down on Week One, Day 2. Reflect on that list and revise if necessary.

TALENTS

Since we're born with innate talents, they are probably the same today as on Day 2. However, this journey may have uncovered some hidden talents you didn't realize you had. If that's the case, be sure to identify them today.

INTERESTS

Compare your initial list of interests with how you feel today.

- Have your interests shifted? Do any need to be removed from your list?

- Are there new interests you've uncovered since starting the program?

- Have you found new hobbies or activities that inspire you or bring more joy, awe, or zest into your life?

- Write down things you dream about, like exploring exotic locations around the world or flying to the moon. Dream Big!

I'm the master of my shift!

AFFIRMATION

I am constantly discovering new interests and passions that bring me joy.

WEEK FIFTEEN ━━━━━━━━━━━ **DAY 2**

Unveiling Your True Self

Create an updated list of interests and talents. Highlight any new talents or interests you've discovered.

_____
_____
_____
_____
_____
_____
_____
_____
_____
_____
_____
_____
_____
_____
_____

Believe in your infinite potential.
Your only limitations are those you set upon yourself.
– Roy T. Bennett

WEEK FIFTEEN

Who Am I Now?

DAY 3

My Roles in Life

Review Week One, Day 3 to determine if the roles you identified are still relevant today.

- Have any of your roles changed?

- Are there roles you've let go of or new ones you've embraced?

- Have any relationships shifted for better or worse?

- Do you need to eliminate any of the roles on your list that are not helping advance your personal development?

- What roles do you need to add to help you achieve your dream, further your personal development, or assist in moving your career forward?

Adjust your roles based on your current priorities. Identify any roles that need nurturing, boundaries that need to be set, or roles that need to be eliminated.

I'm the master of my shift!

AFFIRMATION

I embrace the roles that enrich my life and empower me to grow personally and professionally.

Week Fifteen — Day 3

Unveiling Your True Self

DEFINE YOUR ROLES

ROLE	PERSON or GROUP	PROS	CONS	SCORE

I am the light that reflects all things in my world!
– Rev. Christian Sorensen, D.D.

WEEK FIFTEEN

Who Am I Now?

DAY 4

My Core Values

Refer back to core values from Week One, Day 4.

Remember, core values:
- are your personal code of conduct;
- define your ethical boundaries;
- underscore what you stand for;
- represent your unique essence; and
- guide your behavior and interactions personally and professionally.

Review the core values you identified and ask:
- Are these values still the foundation of your life?
- Have new values emerged that you want to focus on?
- How well are you living in alignment with your values today compared to when you started?

I didn't share my core values with you on day 4 because I didn't want to influence your discovery of your own values. However, at this point in the program, I feel it's appropriate to share my values, which are integrity, authenticity, gratitude, and kindness.

Authenticity Gratitude
Grace Loyalty Kindness Resilience FAIRNESS
HONESTY Humility
generosity Love responsibility Respect
Courage ACCOUNTABILITY
empathy Open-minded Compassion
Integrity Perseverance

I'm the master of my shift!

AFFIRMATION

I affirm my core values as guiding principles that shape my actions and decisions.

WEEK FIFTEEN — — — — — — — — — — — — **DAY 4**

Unveiling Your True Self

Confirm or update your list of core values.

_____

_____

_____

_____

_____

_____

_____

_____

_____

_____

_____

_____

_____

_____

_____

Values are like fingerprints. Nobody's are the same,
but you leave them all over everything you do.
– Elvis Presley

WEEK FIFTEEN

Who Am I Now?

DAY 5

My Strengths and Weaknesses

It's time to review your strengths and weaknesses. Review Week One, Day 5 to determine if you need to make any adjustments.

- What do you do effortlessly that others often struggle with, and how can you lean into these strengths more effectively in your daily life?

- What challenges or situations consistently make you feel uncomfortable or inadequate, and what steps can you take to grow in these areas?

- When have you received compliments or recognition that surprised you, what does that reveal about strengths you might overlook in yourself?

- Which of your weaknesses has taught you the most valuable lessons, and how can you use those lessons to improve yourself?

I'm the master of my shift!

AFFIRMATION

I honor my strengths as gifts that empower me to make a positive impact on the world and embrace my weaknesses as opportunities for growth and self-discovery.

WEEK FIFTEEN — **DAY 5**

Unveiling Your True Self

Adjust the list of your strengths and weaknesses as necessary. Make a plan for surrounding yourself with people who build up the areas you identified as weaknesses and how you will use your strengths to support others.

Our strength grows out of our weaknesses.
– Ralph Waldo Emerson

WEEK FIFTEEN

Who Am I Now?

DAY 6

My Support Team

It's time to reassess the people on your support team. Review the team you identified on Week One, Day 6 to determine if you need to make any changes to your team.

- Do these people still support your goals?

- Are there individuals you need to add to your team for further growth?

- Are there any relationships that may no longer serve you or require boundaries? If so, do they need to be removed from your team?

Action   Adjust the members of your support team as necessary. Reach out to your team members to thank them, strengthen your connections, and confirm their participation moving forward.

I'm the master of my shift!

AFFIRMATION

I am blessed with awesome people on my support team!

Week Fifteen — DAY 6

Unveiling Your True Self

MY SUPPORT TEAM

NAME	RELATIONSHIP	HOW TO THEY HELP?	SCORE
EXAMPLE: Marci	My mother	She is my biggest cheerleader and supports my dreams.	10

Find a group of people who challenge and inspire you,
spend a lot of time with them, and it will change your life.
– Amy Poehler

WEEK FIFTEEN

Who Am I Now?

DAY 7

My Personal Mission Statement

Review the personal mission statement you wrote on Week One, Day 7.

- Does it still reflect who you are and what you want?

- Have your goals or sense of purpose shifted?

- How well does your mission statement guide you today?

As with core values, I purposely didn't share my mission statement with you at the beginning of our journey. However, in the interest of transparency, here are the long and short versions of my personal mission statement:

- With integrity as my foundation, authenticity as my essence, gratitude as my attitude, and kindness as my soul, my mission is to make a meaningful difference in the lives of others by leaving a legacy of love, compassion, and positivity in the world.

- To make a meaningful difference in the lives of others by leaving a legacy of love, compassion, and positivity in the world.

I'm the master of my shift!

AFFIRMATION

I embrace my personal mission statement as a source of inspiration, motivation, and purpose, empowering me to live authentically and make a positive impact in the world.

WEEK FIFTEEN   **DAY 7**

Unveiling Your True Self

Confirm or revise your mission statement. Be sure it's clear, inspiring, and aligns with your values and the life you envision.

Your personal mission statement is a bold affirmation of your purpose in life.
– Stephen Covey

My Masterplan

MY MASTERPLAN

Today is a day of celebration! You will reflect on your journey and outline your personal masterplan to solidify your plan for continued success. Begin by reflecting on the following questions:

- What are your key takeaways from this journey?

- What new habits and thought patterns will you continue to practice?

- What has changed in your life?

- Do you feel more empowered today than when you began this journey? If not, why not, and what changes do you need to make moving forward?

- What are your next steps in your personal empowerment journey?

WRITE YOUR MASTERPLAN

Your final step is to write your masterplan with the following sections:

My Dream
If I could do anything in life, knowing I would not fail, I would ____

My Interests

My Talents

My Strengths

My Weaknesses

My Support Team

My Core Values

My Personal Mission Statement

In addition to the elements you defined during this journey (your dream, interests, talents, strengths, weaknesses, support team, core values, and personal mission statement), here are some additional components to consider:

Vision Statement
A broad statement that outlines what you want your life to look like in the long term. It can be an inspiring reminder of where you want to go.

Legacy
What impact do you want to leave behind? This can include how you want to be remembered by your family, community, or profession.

I'm the master of my shift!

AFFIRMATION

I'm the master of my shift and I choose happiness and success!

MY MASTERPLAN

Goals
Write specific, measurable, achievable, relevant, and time-bound (SMART) goals that align with your vision and mission. These can be divided into short-term (1 year), mid-term (3 years), and long-term (5+ years) goals.

Financial Goals and Plan
Establish financial objectives such as savings, investments, and budgeting that align with your larger life goals.

Self-Care and Wellness (Review Week 4, Day 6, Self-Compassion)

Include a section dedicated to how you will take care of your physical, mental, and emotional well-being so you can live your best life.

Time Management (Review Week 5, Day 4, Time Management)

Include your strategy for allocating your time effectively to ensure that while you're working toward your goals, you maintain balance in other areas of life.

Habits
In addition to the daily routine you established during this program, identify any new habits you would like to develop to support your goals and personal development.

Opportunities for Growth
Identify areas where you can stretch yourself, step out of your comfort zone, or learn something new. This can include educational goals, skill development, or overcoming fears.

Obstacles and Challenges
Anticipate potential obstacles that might stand in your way and strategize how to overcome them. Being prepared for setbacks can help with resilience.

Celebrating and Rewarding Milestones
Recognize key achievements along the way and plan how you will reward yourself for reaching important milestones to stay motivated.

Action
- Write your masterplan.
- Practice the Daily Routine every day!
- Live life from A to Z—in Awe and with Zest!

Embrace your heart's purpose now!
– Dr. Roger Teel

EPILOGUE

Well, here we are at the end of *The Shift Code*. Or is it really the beginning? You've persevered through fifteen weeks of self-reflection, mindset shifts, and probably more sticky notes filled with affirmations than you thought possible. You've dug deep, challenged old beliefs, reframed your thoughts, and maybe even had a few "aha" moments along the way. And now, you stand at the threshold of something incredible—your "shifted" life.

Remember all the way back to week one when I asked you to dream big? You probably had some doubts like, "Can I really pull this off?" Maybe you still do. But you've already accomplished the hardest part. You showed up for yourself, day after day, even when it felt like your chatter brain was being a total jerk. You practiced mindfulness, kindness, patience, and persistence, and let's not forget, you learned to laugh at yourself when things didn't go exactly as planned, which happens to everyone.

You've done the work, but this isn't a one-and-done deal. The beauty of *The Shift Code* is that it's a living, breathing part of you now. You can revisit these techniques whenever life throws you a curveball (and it will). Whether you're chasing a new dream, fine-tuning your personal mission statement, or just trying to get through a tough Monday, you've got the tools. You're equipped to handle whatever comes your way.

So, what now? Whether you take on a new challenge, repeat this program, or just sit back and appreciate how far you've come, that's up to you—you're the shift master. You hold the map, the keys, and the power to keep evolving.

Before we part ways, I want to remind you of something important. Life is messy. Progress isn't linear, and you'll have days where it feels like you're back to square one. That's okay. Shift happens (pun absolutely intended), and you now have the tools to roll with it. You are resilient and, most importantly, capable of living your best life!

So go ahead, embrace the shifts, big and small. Celebrate your wins, laugh off your setbacks, and keep moving forward. You're the master of your shift. And that, my friend, is something to celebrate every single day.

Stay shifted, stay awesome, and keep shining!

With gratitude and a whole lot of high-fives,
Gay

RESOURCES

Beckwith, M. (n.d.). *Michael Beckwith.* https://www.michaelbeckwith.com/

Centers for Spiritual Living. (n.d.). *Centers for Spiritual Living.* https://csl.org/

Dyer, W. (2004). *The Power of Intention: Learning to Co-create Your World Your Way.* Hay House.

Dyer, W. (2007). *Change Your Thoughts-Change Your Life. Living the Wisdom of the Tao.* Hay House.

Emergenetics. (n.d.). https://emergenetics.com/

Gratitude Revealed. (n.d.). https://gratituderevealed.com/

Greater Good Science Center. (n.d.). *Greater Good Science Center.* University of California, Berkeley. https://ggsc.berkeley.edu/

Hanh, T. N. (1999). *The Miracle of Mindfulness: An Introduction to the Practice of Meditation.* Beacon Press.

Helmstetter, S. (1990). *What to Say When You Talk to Your Self.* Pocket Books.

Holmes, E. (1938). *The Science of Mind.* Tarcher Perigee.

Ernest Holmes Science of Mind Archives. (n.d.). *Ernest Holmes Science of Mind Archives.* https://scienceofmindarchives.com/about-ernest-holmes/

Institute for Health and Human Potential (IHHP). (n.d.). *EI360™ Assessment.* https://www.ihhp.com/

International Forgiveness Institute. (n.d.). *International Forgiveness Institute.* https://internationalforgiveness.com/

Logothetis, L. (n.d.). *The Kindness Diaries.* https://www.leonlogothetis.com/

Markkula Center for Applied Ethics. (n.d.). *Markkula Center for Applied Ethics.* Santa Clara University. https://www.scu.edu/ethics/

Matee, N. (n.d.). *Recycle Build: Plastic Bricks.* Recycle Rebuild. https://www.recyclerebuild.org/

RESOURCES

Mindful. (n.d.). https://www.mindful.org/

Pew Research Center. (2023, December 7). *Spirituality among Americans.* https://www.pewresearch.org/religion/2023/12/07/spirituality-among-americans/

Random Acts of Kindness Foundation. (n.d.). *Random Acts of Kindness Foundation.* https://www.randomactsofkindness.org/

Rath, T. (2007). *StrengthsFinder 2.0.* Gallup Press.

Simply Psychology: Maslow's Hierarchy of Needs. (n.d.). https://www.simplypsychology.org/maslow.html

Sorensen, C. (n.d.). *Christian Sorensen Inspires.* https://www.christiansorenseninspires.com/

Teel, R. (n.d.). *Dr. Roger Teel.* https://rogerteel.com/

The Virtues Project. (n.d.). https://www.virtuesproject.com/

UCLA Health Mindful Awareness Research Center. (n.d.). *UCLA Health Mindful Awareness Research Center.* https://www.uclahealth.org/uclamindful

VIA Institute on Character. (n.d.). *VIA Institute on Character.* https://www.viacharacter.org/